MODERN HANDGUNS

MODERN HANDGUNS

ROBERT ADAM

THE
APPLE
PRESS

A QUINTET BOOK

Published by The Apple Press
6 Blundell Street
London N7 9BH

ISBN 1-85076-127-2

This book was designed and produced by
Quintet Publishing Limited
6 Blundell Street
London N7 9BH

Creative Director: Peter Bridgewater
Art Designer: Ian Hunt
Designer Stuart Walden
Project Editor: Shaun Barrington
Editor: Henrietta Wilkinson
Photographer: Paul Forrester

Typeset in Great Britain by
Central Southern Typesetters, Eastbourne
Manufactured in Hong Kong by
Regent Publishing Services Limited
Printed in Hong Kong by
Leefung-Asco Printers Limited

CONTENTS

WHAT IS A MODERN HANDGUN?

The modern handgun was born with the expiry of Colt's patents in 1849 and 1857 which ended his stranglehold on the development of self-indexing, revolving cylinder handguns in Great Britain and America. In 1856, Horace Smith and Daniel Wesson formed the American company that still bears their name – Smith & Wesson – in order to develop and subsequently manufacture a revolver using the French metallic rimfire cartridge. In so doing, they started the American firearms industry on a half century of rapid evolution.

Even before then, however, handguns had come a long way since the term *handgonne* was first used to describe small hand- or shoulder-held cannon in the 14th century. Large, heavy weapons, these were usually fully stocked and often required additional support for aiming and firing. The invention and naming of the pistol – a distinctive short-barrelled firearm without a shoulder stock – has been accredited to Caminellea Vitelli, a 16th-century Italian gunmaker residing in Pistoia, near Florence in Italy. Other historians claim that the word pistol is derived from the Bohemian word *pistal,* used for a smoker's pipe, and yet more believe the origins to be the Italian description *pistallo,* used for a saddle's pommel over which an early handgun would have been slung.

Today, the term "handgun" is reserved for pistols and revolvers, and "smallarms" is used for all shoulder- and hand-fired weapons of less than 15mm bore. "Pistol" is sometimes used to describe all handguns, but I prefer to separate out revolving cylinder handguns (revolvers) and pepperboxes. "Pistol" is better used for single-shot and static multi-barrelled or self-loading "semi automatic" handguns.

Handguns are principally used as personal defensive arms, but the German Rieter cavalry used pistols with devastating effect to attack the French at the battle of Renty in 1544. Handguns have been used more recently for covert and special military operations where their concealability and light weight have proved to be vital.

■ WHEEL LOCK

The early pistols of the 16th and 17th centuries were often called "daggs", single-barrelled pieces loaded with a heavy lead ball, and utilizing a compact wheel lock to fire them. The wheel lock, invented around 1510, used a spring to drive a small wheel against iron pyrites held in a clamp. The resulting shower of sparks following release of the trigger ignited the gunpowder in the flash pan, which in turn ignited the main charge. Wheel-lock ignition was most efficient and reliable compared to its predecessor, the match lock, and made the pistol a feasible arm to be carried concealed for protection because of its small size.

■ FLINTLOCK

The wheel lock was expensive to manufacture, however, and at the end of the 16th century the cheaper snaphaunce lock was produced, which was developed and refined into the flintlock in the 17th century. Handguns were still principally simple single-barrelled weapons, although some horse pistols were made with duplex double trigger wheel locks to fire two barrels. Flintlock double pistols were occasionally made to fire both barrels together with a single-trigger pull. At the end of the 17th century an Italian three-barrelled revolving flintlock pistol was made, but this required the barrels to be turned by hand and the flash pan re-primed before each was fired.

■ PERCUSSION

The discovery in Europe of mercury fulminate, a chemical salt which explodes when struck, lead to the development of the percussion cap at the beginning of the 19th century. The percussion cap made reliable lightweight repeating arms a possibility for the first time in 500 years of firearms development. Flint lock revolving barrel pepperboxes were redesigned, and single-barrelled multi-chambered revolvers were developed.

■ PERCUSSION PEPPERBOX AND REVOLVER PATENTS

In 1836 the Darling Brothers were granted the first US pepperbox patent, the same year as Colt's original US revolver patent. In 1837 Ethan Allen patented his trigger-cocking self-indexing pepperbox, the same year that Samuel Colt produced his first Pocket Model Paterson Revolver (No. 1) in ·28 in calibre. Colt used his hammer-indexing patent to block competition from the Massachusetts Arms Company in a celebrated court case in 1851, and earlier by threat of action against the Springfield Arms Company.

■ TURRET REVOLVERS

Turret revolvers were made by Cochran in the late 1830s and in 1851 by P. W. Porter. These were both ungainly and

Left British Webleys and American Colt New Service revolvers in ·455 in calibre both saw service in the Great War (1914–18). The basic design of Colt's double action revolvers has not changed since then.

Below Robert Adams produced a trigger cocking percussion revolver which he exhibited at the Great Exhibition in 1851.

unpopular, since unfired chambers would point back at the shooter and if detonated by accident could result in the demise of the revolver's owner as well as his aggressor – as indeed happened to Porter when he was demonstrating his weapon during a US military trial.

■ ROBERT ADAMS

Colt had patented his revolver design in England in 1835, but the patent expired in 1849. It was not used for manufacture, only to block competition, and London gunmaker Robert Adams soon produced a solid frame trigger-cocking cap-and-ball revolver which he exhibited in 1851 alongside Colt's open frame single-action designs at the Great Exhibition in London.

■ ROLLIN WHITE AND SMITH & WESSON

On April 3, 1855, Rollin White obtained the patent number 12608 in the United States for a revolver which included cylinders which were bored through from end to end in its design. In 1856, having departed from the Volcanic Arms Company, Smith and Wesson joined forces in Massachusetts, US, in order to acquire and exploit the bored-through cylinder part of the patent. Volcanic Arms had been started by Smith and Wesson to manufacture Smith's improved patent lever action rifle and pistol. Volcanic Arms later became the Winchester Repeating Arms Company, manufacturing Henry and Browning-designed lever action rifles and carbines. Owning the Rollin White patent put Smith & Wesson in a commanding position for handgun manufacture when Colt's US patent on the revolving cylinder expired in 1857.

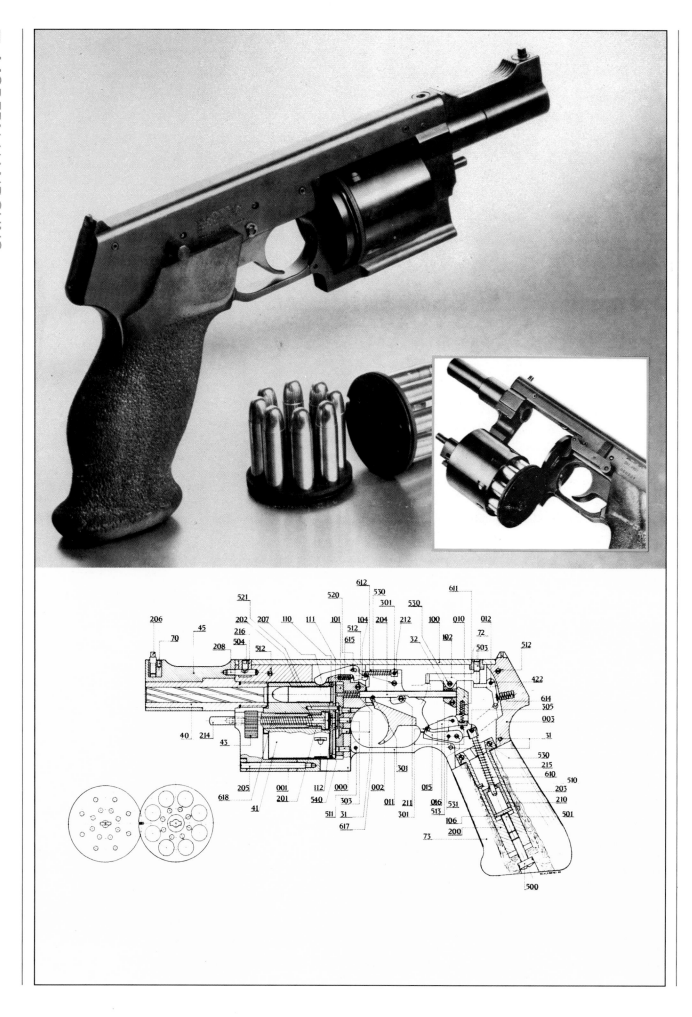

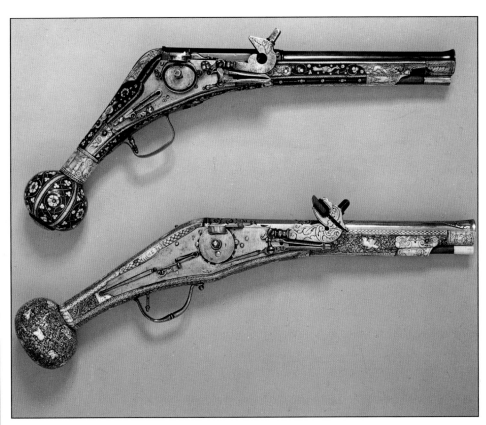

■ Left *The wheel lock pistol made it possible to carry a concealed pistol for defence in the 16th century.*

■ Opposite *The Italian Mateba has been the only radical redesign of a revolver in the 20th century. Chambered for eight rounds of ·38 Special, the Mateba has a very low bore line for precision shooting.*

Metallic cartridges used in a bored-through cylinder revolver created a breech loading handgun which could be rapidly fired and rapidly reloaded. By using the patent, Smith & Wesson became the only significant manufacturers of metallic cartridge revolvers, and because of the demand they created, were soon two years behind on deliveries. For the 12 years of the patent's protection, around 50 American gunmakers had begun producing revolvers, but they were mainly limited to the cap-and-ball design for which there was great demand during the American Civil War in the early 1860s. The Civil War also ended the manufacture of pepperboxes, since the revolver had now become lighter, cheaper, more powerful and more accurate.

The Rollin White patent expired in 1869, creating the freedom to manufacture and sell new cartridge revolver designs; this opportunity was seized by manufacturers who had survived the Civil War, and a number set up in the 1870s.

■ COLT'S PEACEMAKER

Samuel Colt died in 1862 but his company survived, and in 1872 Colt's factory at Hartford, Connecticut, US, produced one of the most famous cartridge revolvers of all time, the Single Action Army. Also known as the Peacemaker, the Single Action Army remained in production until 1940 after a manufacturing run of over 350,000. The Peacemaker was Colt's first solid frame revolver, and had rod ejection which pushed out the fired cases one at a time. Colt re-started production of the single action Peacemaker in 1955 due to consumer demand.

■ BEAUMONT-ADAMS

So great was the American love of the single action Peacemaker that it was left to Europeans to develop and perfect the double action revolver, which could be fired by trigger-cocking, or by first hand cocking. Robert Adams' trigger-cocking percussion revolver had been beaten by Colt's single action handgun for a British Army and Royal Navy contract in 1851, but in 1854 the British Army adopted the Beaumont-Adams double action percussion revolver for use in the Crimean War. The Beaumont-Adams was later converted to breech loading. Adams' designs were used in the US by the Massachusetts Arms Co. on their Adams Patent Revolvers, five shooters in ·31 and ·36 calibres made between 1857 and 1861.

■ WEBLEY

In 1867, the Webley brothers secured an official contract to supply the Royal Irish Constabulary with six shot ·422 in double action cartridge revolvers. In 1877, Webley manufactured a breaktop self-extracting revolver incorporating the Pryse patents for the same. The ·422 Webley was adopted 10 years later as the British service pistol, beginning an association which lasted intermittently through two world wars and several calibres until the revolver was superseded by the self-loading Browning pistol in 1957.

■ AMERICAN DOUBLE ACTION

Colt's first double action revolver, the Lightening, was made in 1877, and Smith & Wesson's first were in 1880,

■ *George Luger developed the Borchardt into a more compact and reliable pistol which was adopted by the German Services in 1905 and 1908. The Luger itself was used as a model for the Finnish-designed Lahti service pistol (**below**) in 1935, which did away with the Luger's temperamental toggle lock.*

■ *Below The Mauser "Broomhandle" Model 1896 used a powerful 7·63mm cartridge developed from the ammunition used in Borchardt's pistol.*

the ·32 and ·38 Double Action First Model breaktops. Both companies were preceded in the US by Ethan Allen's sons-in-law, who patented their Forehand and Wadsworth Double action ·32 rimfire revolver in 1871 and by C. S. Pettengill's pocket revolvers which were made by Rodgers, Spencer & Co in the late 1850s and early 1860s.

The Iver Johnson Company introduced the transfer bar safety lock in 1896, which meant that their revolvers' hammer could only contact the firing pin if the trigger was pulled back to the correct position; this eliminated the need to carry a revolver with the hammer down on an empty chamber.

■ END OF REVOLVER DEVELOPMENT

In 1896 Smith & Wesson produced their first swing-out cylinder revolver, the ·32 Hand Ejector 1st Model DA, and in 1899 brought out the ·38 Hand Ejector 1st Model DA which featured a frame-mounted cylinder latch. Whilst there have been changes in frame size, cylinder locking points, and construction materials since the turn of the

20th century, the current Smith & Wesson revolvers do not exhibit any significant design initiatives over the models of the early 1900s.

Similarly, Colt's Model 1889 Navy Double Action swing-out cylinder revolver set in stone most of their basic revolver design ideas for the next 90 years.

The escalating military conflicts and social unrest in the second half of the 19th century focussed the impetus for arms development in Europe. Revolver design reached an elegant peak in England in 1896 when George Vincent Fosbery patented an automatic revolver which was later refined and adapted by Webley and Scott and sold as the Webley-Fosbery, based on their standard hinge-framed revolver.

■ MATEBA REVOLVER

With the exception of the Italian Mateba eight shot revolver produced in the 1980s, the main improvements in revolvers have been in the powerful new calibres that they are chambered for, and in the materials used to make them.

The Mateba ·38 featured a cylinder mounted in front of the trigger mechanism instead of above it, giving a very low bore line, preferred for target shooting. This also makes the pistol long and muzzle-heavy, reducing its suitability for service or defence use.

■ SMOKELESS POWDERS AND SELF-LOADING PISTOL

There had been a number of attempts at producing a working self-loading pistol in the 19th century but it was the introduction of high pressure nitrocellulose and nitro-glycerine-based "smokeless" propellants which made self-loading operation feasible. Prior to that, the thick, corrosive residue left by gunpowder (black powder) on firing soon fouled and jammed any weapon made to the fine tolerances required for self-loading. Gun cotton and nitro-glycerine had been discovered by 1848 and a gunpowder substitute, made from nitrated wood, was found by the Prussian Schultz in 1865. But it was not until Nobel produced stable nitroglycerine in the 1870s that "smokeless" powder could be safely used in smallarms ammunition. The French adopted Vielle smokeless powder in 1886 for their 8mm Lebel rifle, and in 1889 British Cordite was perfected.

■ SCHONBERGER

The first working automatic pistol to be produced is believed to have been the 1890–92 Schonberger, made at the Steyr arms factory in Germany. Based on the Laumann mechanical repeater, the pistol is understood to have used the primer set back – which occurs on initial firing – to initiate unlocking of the breech, and permit straightforward blowback operation. Unfortunately, no ammunition has survived, so the operational theory cannot be proved.

■ BORCHARDT

Hugo Borchardt was a German emigré to the United States in 1865 and worked for a number of arms manufacturers, including Colt, Sharps, and Winchester. Borchardt designed several firearms and innovations which pre-dated many of those of the major manufacturers, but few were ever made due to political deals and trade-offs between his employers and their competitors. Borchardt returned to Europe in 1882 and joined the employment of Ludwig Lowe in Berlin in 1892. Lowe had established himself in the late 1870s by manufacturing Smith & Wesson ·44 Russian revolvers under licence for the Russian army. In 1893 Borchardt patented a toggle-jointed self-loading pistol based on the Maxim machine gun, and supervized its manufacture by Lowe in Berlin.

■ LUGER

The Borchardt was frail and clumsy, and another employee of Ludwig Lowe, George Luger, improved Borchardt's de-

sign. Luger's Parabellum pistol, in 7·65mm calibre, was sold in Europe in 1900 and in the United States in 1904, after overcoming objections from Colt and Browning. The original 7·65mm calibre was upgraded to 9mm and offered to the British Army in 1902, but they turned it down. The German Navy approved the design in 1905, and the adoption of the pistol by the German Army in 1908 started the 9mm Luger round on its journey to becoming the most popular service pistol ammunition in use today.

■ BERGMANN

Another self-loading pistol was patented in 1893 by Theodor Bergmann Waffenfabrik of Suhl, Germany. This was a 5mm blowback design which incorporated some of the features of Bergmann's first pistol patent of 1892 which he filed jointly with Otto Brauswetter, a Hungarian watchmaker. Bergmann also employed Louis Schmeisser, who designed a number of pistols and sub-machine guns for him.

■ MAUSER 1896

The rifle makers Mauser produced the Zig Zag revolver in 1878, which rotated the cylinder by using a moving pin running in the frame sliding along a Z-shaped groove in the cylinder. The revolver was not adopted by the military authorities and the factory turned its attention to self-loading pistols. After a number of false starts with very complicated pistols, the Military Pistol of 1896 was eventually a success. Nicknamed "the Broomhandle" after its distinctive grip, the Model 1896 did not win any military contracts, but still became a very popular pistol. The Broomhandle's ammunition magazine is located in front of the trigger guard, a design perpetuated today in target pistols. This allows modern pistols to have a low bore line in relation to the grip, making recoil easier to control.

■ JOHN MOSES BROWNING

The most prolific arms designer of the last century was the American John Moses Browning, who designed many of Winchester rifles and an early machine gun made by Colt. Browning then turned his attention to self-loading pistols and Colt made its first "automatic" in 1900 using Browning's 1897 patent. Browning had struck up a commercial relationship with Fabrique National d'Armes de Guerre (FN) of Belgium at the turn of the century, the collaboration producing their first Browning pistol, the Model 1900 in 7·62mm (·32). FN next produced the Model 1903, a larger handgun in a new calibre (9mm Browning Long), one of the most powerful cartridges successfully used in a lightweight straight-blowback pistol. Colt and FN made a number of similar pistols using Browning's designs, having agreed not to compete against each other in the same markets.

■ COLT 1911

Browning designed a locked breech self-loading pistol which Colt made as the Model 1905 pistol in ·45 Rimless Smokeless calibre for the US army. The 1905 was developed into the Colt 1911 which fired the ·45 Automatic Colt Pistol cartridge. The basic 1911-type pistol was improved slightly after the Great War (1914–1918) and re-named the 1911 A1. Over 2.5 million 1911 and 1911 A1s were made before it was replaced as the US-issue sidearm by the Beretta 92F 9mm pistol in 1985, having had a service life of 74 years. Colt still use the 1911 design for their 9mm, ·38

Super and ·45 ACP pistols, and in 1987 they launched another version in the new 10mm calibre.

■ BROWNING HIGH POWER

The Browning Model 1935 in 9mm Luger, also known as the GP35 or High Power, was developed from locked breech designs Browning left when he died in 1926. The designs were patented by FN in 1927, and following its launch in 1935, the GP35 became the most popular military pistol of the non-communist countries.

Browning's domination of self-loading pistol design is

■ *Opposite* The influence of John Moses Browning on self-loading pistol design spanned a quarter of a century until his death in 1926. His designs were simple and reliable and were sold by Colt in the US and FN in Europe under the Browning name. His last design was refined to become the Browning GP35 (**bottom right**). Chambered for 9mm Luger, it is still in service today.

■ *Right* The up-to-date Heckler & Koch P9S uses roller locking of the breech similar to the mechanism used on H&K's rifles.

still apparent today; many of the "new" pistols launched retain his recoil-operated delayed blowback principles. Modern pistols often use the chamber block to lock the barrel into the ejector port, instead of relying on locking lugs ahead of the chamber.

■ HECKLER & KOCH P7

A new modern design, the German Heckler & Koch P7 9mm self-loading pistol utilizes propellant gas to aid its operation. 9mm Luger is too powerful a cartridge to be used with ease in a lightweight, straight blowback pistol. To reduce the pressure on the breech, the P7 uses a gas-retarded action, where some propellant gas is bled off from the barrel into a cylinder machined in the frame, into which the recoil spring guide fits. The gas pressure on firing pushes against the recoil spring guide, delaying the rearwards movement of the slide. When the bullet leaves the barrel, the gas pressure in the cylinder drops and the slide can then recoil, now being controlled by recoil spring. The P7 also uses squeeze-cocking, where the pressure of the shooter's grip cocks the hammer/striker prior to firing. If the grip is released, the pistol decocks. This system eliminates the need for safety catches or a combined double and single action trigger mechanism.

The Heckler & Koch engineers adapted the roller-locked breech from their self-loading rifles and used it to slow down breech and slide movement in a different form of delayed blowback on their P9S pistols.

■ GAS OPERATED PISTOLS

Gas operation makes self-loading pistols bulky and complex, as well as requiring a very powerful cartridge to generate enough gas to cycle the action. Most have not made it past the drawing board, and those which do have limited commercial success. The Wildey pistol has made it to the market with two calibre options, both produced specifically for it, the ·45 Winchester Magnum and the 9mm Winchester

Magnum. The Wildey utilizes a rotating breech block as well as gas operation, a feature shared by the Israel Military Industries' Desert Eagle Pistol, which fires the ·44 Magnum and ·357 Magnum rimmed revolver cartridges. Both of these large handguns were designed with handgun hunting (and the growing metallic silhouette shooting sports) in mind, rather than for self-defence. AMT's Auto-mag II uses a gas assisted action with a rimfire ·22 WMR calibre.

■ BURST FIRE PISTOLS

Once the principals of self-loading operation in handguns had been mastered, attempts were soon made to make pistols fully automatic. The problem, as Browning found at the turn of the century, is that small handguns are uncontrollable in fully automatic fire, with most of the ammunition wasted on the sky. After the Second World War, the Russians developed the Stetchkin pistol which had selective fire capability with a shoulder stock attached. This was

■ *The Israeli Desert Eagle is a massive self-loading pistol using the propellant gas to cycle the action.*

The Desert Eagle is chambered for two revolver cartridges, ·357 Magnum and ·44 Magnum.

■ *Heckler & Koch's VP70 pistol can be set to fire three shot bursts with the shoulder stock attached.*

intended to replace both the machine pistol and the defensive handgun, but has now been dropped in favour of dedicated weapons. In Europe, Heckler & Koch and Beretta have both produced elegant burst fire self-loading pistols, which can fire up to three shots with one pull of the trigger. The H&K VP 70 can only be used for burst fire with a shoulder stock, and the Beretta 93R is also best used with one to maintain control. The disadvantage of burst fire operation is that a small, 20-round magazine is soon emptied, and it is preferable to use burst fire in heavier, high magazine capacity, or closed bolt machine pistols.

■ BLIND ALLEYS

Firearms designers have travelled up other blind alleys in the quest for a better handgun. One notable failure was the Gyrojet, which fired tiny rockets from a lightweight pistol. The Gyrojet's range was limited and its accuracy appalling, which reduced its appeal. Another non-starter was the Dardick open chamber pistol in which triangular ammunition was swept up from the magazine by a rotor to line up with the barrel, the chamber being formed by the pistol's rotor and topstrap.

■ TODAY'S POPULAR HANDGUNS

Following the early rapid advances in handgun design and development, it now takes considerable time for new handgun ideas to be accepted. Five types have survived the passage of time and remain with us today – single shot, derringers, revolvers, self-loading pistols, and assault pistols.

Strong, single shot pistols are now chambered for high performance rifle cartridges, and are used for sporting target shooting and hunting.

Derringers have always been an extremely close-range handgun, used for defence. Since they usually have two fixed barrels it is easy to chamber them for range of calibres from ·22 rimfire up to ·45–70 and ·223/5·56mm.

The revolver with the double action trigger is very popular, and is used for law enforcement, personal defence and target shooting; its predecessor, with a single action hand-cocked trigger, is now used with powerful new calibres for hunting.

The lightweight self-loading pistol has been favoured by armies since the First World War, and is now being used for law enforcement and defence. Sophisticated small calibre self-loading pistols are used for international target shooting.

The final group, the closed bolt assault pistol, has been derived from small open bolt machine pistols, and share many of their design features, including similar high capacity ammunition magazines. The principal users of assault pistols are law enforcement agencies.

■ *Opposite Beretta's Model 93R also has a selector to permit burst fire. Accuracy is improved by using a shoulder stock.*

■ *J D Jones of SSK Industries converts single shot Thompson/Center Contenders into even more potent hunting "Handcannons".*

DEVELOPMENTS IN MATERIALS FOR HANDGUNS

At the turn of the century, the transition from black powder to nitrocellulose propellants in handgun ammunition demanded stronger raw materials and better construction of the weapons themselves. Black powder was dirty and corrosive when burned, and generated low pressure in firearms' chambers and breeches. Even small quantities of smokeless powders produced pressures approaching double those of the old gunpowders, and many early firearms exploded when they were inadvertently used with smokeless ammunition. For new handguns, better grades of steel and generally heavier construction were necessary to reap the improved performance benefits of the new propellants. Where brass had been used previously for frames, this was replaced with steel.

WARTIME MANUFACTURE

The escalating European military conflicts of the 20th century created a demand for firearms on a scale previously unseen. With little time to develop new methods of construction before the First World War, the handguns used were produced in much the same way as they had been for the previous 20 years; the only use of rubber and early plastics was for grips, replacing wood. The principal cost saving in military weapons was in permitting wider manufacturing tolerances and cheapening the finish, using phosphate and crude blacking rather than the high polish and deep blacking used for commercial handguns.

Rearming for the Second World War, however, shortages of steel necessitated a dramatic re-design of fighting weapons. The sub-machine gun had been added to the world's arsenals, and, following Germany's lead with the MP38, these were cheaply made from pressed steel, plastics and wire. The handgun was still regarded as a weapon of last resort, for close quarters defence. The United States issued the steel and wood M1 ·30 carbine to its GIs as a manageable assault weapon, although it still continued to supply the hard kicking 1911A1 pistol to more seasoned soldiers who could control it. Other armies only issued handguns to officers, as defensive weapons for confined spaces such as in tanks or aircraft, or as special silenced versions for covert operations. Simple pressed steel pistols were dropped be-

■ *To survive on the streets, modern handguns use plastics, aluminium alloys and stainless steel in their construction.*

■ *Opposite above For over a century, plating has been a popular protective finish for personal defence handguns which are often carried but infrequently used.*

hind enemy lines for use by resistance organisations. As in the First World War, the main savings with handguns were in finish rather than design and material.

PLATING FOR PROTECTION

The handgun was principally used as a personal defence weapon from the time it was invented, and as such was carried in pockets, holsters or tucked into belts. The proximity of human sweat to a concealed weapon, or of exposure to the elements if carried in an external holster, caused rapid surface corrosion to handguns. Many 19th-century Western revolvers were available in a nickel-plated finish to improve the resistance of the steel frame and cylinders. This tradition was carried over into the 20th century, especially for "pocket pistols", small-framed pistols and revolvers of fairly small calibres which were frequently nickel, chrome or silver plated. Hard chroming, which toughens the surface of steel, has now become commonplace, especially on hunting and IPSC competition pistols.

STAINLESS STEELS

The pressures and stresses involved in firearms precluded the use of any other material than carbon steel for the bulk of their construction for many years. Stainless steel would appear to be an ideal material – being an alloy of iron with up to 20% chromium and 12% nickel – which had been used in industry since the First World War. It was not used for complete firearms, however, until 1965, when Smith & Wesson introduced the Model 60 Chief's Special, a small frame five shot ·38 revolver. This was partly due to the cost of the material and the difficulty of machining it, since tools used on stainless steels wear out up to five times faster than they do when used on mild or even high carbon steels. Another stumbling block was the problem of galling, where stainless steel parts rubbing against each other "pick up"

■ *Smith & Wesson's five shot ·38 in Chiefs Special was the first commercial revolver to be made* *entirely from stainless steel giving it unrivalled resistance to corrosion.*

17

Small specialized manufacturers like Detonics only use high grade stainless steel in the production of their self-loading pistols.

particles from the other, leaving a rough surface. This caused semi automatic pistols to jam unless carefully lubricated with special oils. Stainless steels were also softer than carbon steel and would not hold the edge needed for trigger sears; they would also wear around pivot points, which resulted in revolvers requiring frequent gunsmithing to keep them in tune. It was found that by using different grades of stainless steel for rubbing parts, galling was reduced, and later developments in alloys improved the wear resistance.

·44 AUTO MAG

One of the first wholly stainless self-loading pistols was the ·44 Auto Mag launched in 1971 by Harry Sanford of Pasedena, California. Sanford used cut down ·308 rifle cases to make the ammunition for the Auto Mag. Like many mould-breaking designs, it was not a commercial success in the conservative world of handguns, partly due to the lack of availability of ammunition.

Stainless steel is now a common handgun material, with Smith & Wesson, Colt, Ruger and Walther all making versions of their revolvers or pistols in both stainless and carbon steels. Some of the new US firearms manufacturers, such as Detonics, Freedom Arms, AMT and Randall, only use stainless for their weapons. The Israeli Desert Eagle pistol is now available with a stainless frame, as is the Colt Elite.

The use of stainless steel is appreciated by black powder shooters who delight in using the vintage propellant for

To compete today, handgun manufacturers like Bill Ruger have invested heavily in investment casting of major components.

target shooting, and hunting with old firearms and their replicas. The residue left by black powder on firing is highly corrosive, and many replicas are available in stainless steel versions.

INVESTMENT CASTING

Modern investment or lost wax casting methods have improved the speed and quality of production, as well as reducing costs. Casting has been around since metals were first melted and poured into sand moulds, but cast parts were frequently brittle and porous, unsuitable for lightweight load- or pressure-bearing parts. For these components, the traditional method of manufacture was to take a big lump of high quality steel and machine off anything that did not look like a gun.

Cost saving in handgun production has become as critical as quality; military orders for handguns are based on price and volume, and civilian sales are dropping worldwide due to pressure from domestic anti-gun lobby groups. Computer-controlled lathes and mills can be used for machining, but cheaper ways of production are still needed and investment casting has produced the biggest breakthrough. Lost wax or investment casting starts from an injection-moulded wax "positive" form of the final product. This is coated with a liquid ceramic which is first dried then baked. The wax melts, leaving a perfect "negative" mould into which the molten metal is injected. When set, the ceramic mould is broken off leaving a high quality casting which needs little machining and can be made in a complex shape. The minimal machining required makes the technique most suitable for hard-to-work stainless steels, or any part which would normally need extensive finishing.

RUGER P85

A contemporary pioneer in handgun production technology is Bill Ruger of Sturm Ruger, a company established in New England, US. Now established as a manufacturer of high quality, low priced and rugged handguns making extensive use of investment castings, Ruger has recently launched his first pistol in 9mm Luger, the P85. The operating concepts of the double action pistol are not new, still relying on Browning's turn of the century swinging-link, locked-breech principles. The method of manufacture is fully up to date and Ruger has built a factory in Prescott, Arizona, US, to assemble the new pistol which has been designed with only 50 parts in it. (The "simple" single action Colt 1911 has more than 60 parts, a modern double action revolver, over 70.) The pistol is almost entirely cast – investment-cast chrome-moly steel slide, investment-cast aluminium alloy frame, and the majority of the stainless steel internal parts are investment cast, too. The grips are injection-moulded "Xenoy" plastic, and the pistol has a barrel and chamber made from two pieces screwed together.

ALUMINIUM ALLOYS

The Ruger P85 uses an aluminium alloy frame for lightness. Aluminium is a soft, ductile metal, with similar galling problems to stainless steel when used for rubbing parts. The tensile strength of early alloys was also low, so it could not be used for stressed parts. However, since many handguns are carried a lot and shot very little, some stronger alumi-

nium alloys have been used in the past for pistol and revolver frames. Alloy frames have been particularly popular in those pistols carried day in and day out by bodyguards, such as the Colt Commander 9mm pistol, or the lightweight Charter Arms ·38 and ·44 revolvers. The latest aluminium alloys claim to have a tensile strength far higher than that of steel, and use in frames is becoming common. The impact resistance of aluminium is not yet good enough for slides and heavily stressed barrels; Colt's experiment with lightweight aluminium revolver cylinders for air crew dur-

RUGER P-85

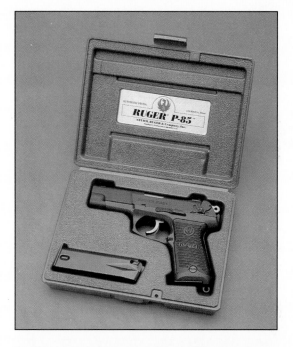

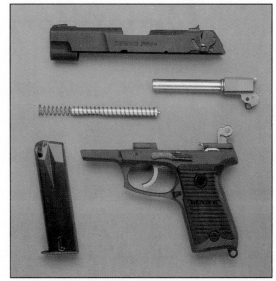

■ Ruger's latest pistol, the 9mm P85, is almost entirely cast, substantially reducing the manufacturing cost.

■ *Light alloy frames are popular for pistols which have to be carried all day. The compact 13-round Smith & Wesson "Mini Gun" has an alloy frame and stainless slide.*

ing the Korean War ended in 1951 when the idea was rejected by US Air Force for ·38 revolvers, and by the public for ·32 and ·22 revolvers in 1955. The American Derringer Corporation has made one of its vast range of derringers in ·38 Spl with a stainless steel frame and aluminium barrels. Smith & Wesson's new lightweight trail pistol, the Model 422, has a high tensile alloy frame and barrel shroud, with pressed steel trigger and action components to produce one of the lowest price, quality, ·22 semi automatics available.

■ *Hämmerli use carbon fibre in their latest target pistol, the Model 280.*

EXOTIC ALLOYS

Other exotic alloys have not been so popular. High tensile manganese bronze has been used in only two handguns, the Century Arms Model 100 Single Action revolver and the Golden Bison Super 6. Beryllium copper has been used for the firing pins in Charter Arms revolvers, and is being investigated for use in pistol frames by Para Ordnance in Canada. Titanium is very strong and extremely light in alloys, but is also extremely expensive. Göncz of California use titanium to line the barrels of their High Tech pistols and this is claimed to reduce barrel wear significantly. Göncz also use very modern coatings to prevent wear in other parts of their pistols, which can also be silenced and used as grenade launchers.

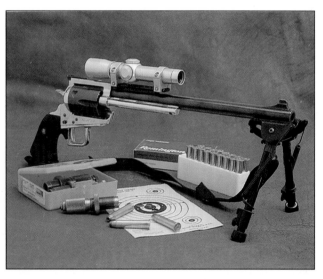

■ ***Above and opposite above*** *Exotic, high-tensile manganese bronze is used for the frame of the single action Century Arms big bore revolvers.*

PLASTIC PISTOLS

Attention is now turning to plastics, carbon fibres and ceramics for new handgun designs. Although rubber, and later plastics, have been used for handgun grips since the 1850s, it took an Austrian engineer who had never designed a pistol before to make extensive structural use of plastics in the Glock 17 pistol. The frame, trigger, and magazines of the Glock are all plastic, which led to media scares worldwide that the Libyans (who had placed an order for 200) would soon be supplying them to terrorists and hijackers since they would not be detectable at airports by metal detectors or X-ray machines. In fact, the Glock still has a steel slide and barrel which contains more metal than some conventional lightweight pocket pistols, and both the Glock and its metal-cased, metal-primed, and metal-bulleted 9mm ammunition are readily detectable by existing security devices.

Hämmerli's Model 280 ·22 target pistol is made with carbon fibre for much of its frame, and indicates the direction target pistol manufacture is heading in. Small bore and target pistols for Olympic and international events are shielded from service constraints of concealability, portability and reliability under field conditions, and while some of their developments – such as the electric release triggers – have not been adopted by mainstream manufacturers, the research can often be refined for service use.

CERAMICS

Ceramics are usually thought of as brittle, temperature resistant compounds, more suited to high tech casting or electronics than handguns. But there are reports that the Eastern Bloc has developed an all plastic gun which fires a ceramic bullet from a plastic case, in an attempt to defeat security devices. In the event of such a product existing, it would probably be a one shot pistol for assassinations rather than something suitable for terrorist activities, which require higher firepower. Plastic-barrelled handguns in the West are used with low pressure non-lethal ammunition in paint guns or cattle marking pistols.

HANDGUN MATERIALS TODAY

The popular revolvers of today, such as the Smith & Wesson Model 686, are made from stainless steel, and the trend for self-loading pistols is for strong alloy frames and carbon steel slides. The high capacity Beretta 92F in 9mm Luger has just such a construction and it has been adopted as the new service pistol in both the United States and France. Single shot pistols are made with investment-cast frames, but their emphasis is on strength rather than cost reduction. Assault pistols make extensive use of pressed steel and plastics, in common with the modern machine pistols they have evolved from.

■ **Above** *The Smith & Wesson Model 686 .357 Magnum is one of the most popular stainless steel revolvers available today.*

■ **Left** *Alloy frames are now common in modern service pistols. Models from the Beretta 92 series in 9mm Luger have been adopted for military and police use in the US and France.*

21

AMMUNITION FOR MODERN HANDGUNS

Modern handgun ammunition started life with the ·22″ Short rimfire cartridge developed by Smith & Wesson in their Model No.1 First Issue Revolver – the first American-made handgun to use the metallic cartridge-type which is still with us today. The rimfire round was far safer and more reliable in revolvers than both the percussion cap-and-ball and the Lefaucheux pinfire cartridge, designed by Houiller in 1836, which had become popular in Europe.

Rimfire ignition uses a ring of priming compound in the folded hollow rim of the case which ignites when crushed by a blow to the rim, in turn starting combustion of the main propellant charge. The idea started from a French patent of 1831 in which priming compound covered the whole of the inside of the cartridge head. Smith & Wesson's rimfire round was developed from the Flobert BB cap of 1845, a very low-powered round used for short-range indoor target practice.

The diminutive ·22 rimfires were short on power, however. Developing only 40 ft.lbs of energy with a 29 grain bullet, they were soon scaled up to larger rimfire calibres reaching ·50 inches for use in single shot pistols and ·44 inches for revolvers. Unfortunately, rimfire cases are inherently weak, since they must be thin enough to be easily crushed with enough force to ignite the priming compound, and so are unsuitable for high pressure ammunition. This soon led to the production of the centrefire cartridge, with a thick brass case head containing a flush central percussion cap to provide ignition. Apart from the remaining ·22 rimfire rounds, centrefire is now the universal design for modern handgun ammunition.

The first revolver rounds were used in handguns with parallel bored cylinders; this meant that the bullet and its cartridge case had to be of the same diameter as the cylinder, which in turn was the same bore as the barrel. Bullets of this type, known as "heeled" or "externally lubricated", are

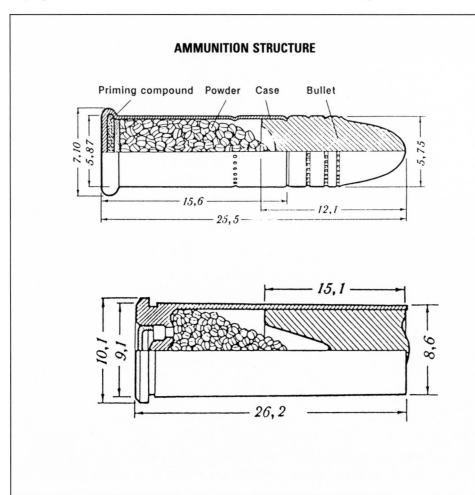

AMMUNITION STRUCTURE

Priming compound   Powder   Case   Bullet

7,10
5,87
15,6
25,5
12,1
5,75

15,1
10,1
9,1
8,6
26,2

■ *Top left* The first modern handguns used ·22 Rimfire cartridges and these are still used today for target shooting matches, vermin control, and inexpensive practice.

■ *Bottom left* Centrefire ammunition in the other calibres has a much stronger case with a central primer. Illustrated is a ·32 target cartridge loaded with a hollow based wadcutter bullet.

■ *Opposite* Ammunition for today's handguns comes in all calibres and types from ·22 RF Short up to ·454 Casull. Just part of the range is illustrated here with a Smith & Wesson Model 52 pistol. The Mod 52 uses a ·38 Special cartridge loaded with a flush flat nosed wadcutter bullet.

held in the case with a small recessed crimp at the base, leaving the bulk of the bullet and its lubricant coating exposed; this design is perpetuated today in the four ·22 rimfire cartridges. By the time the 1873 Colt Peacemaker came on the scene, cartridges had been refined to contain the bullet in an oversized case which enclosed the bullet's grease grooves and the bearing surface, which bites into the barrel's rifling. Smith & Wesson dropped the heeled ·44 American cartridge in favour of ·44 Russian, which eventually grew into the ·44 cartridges available today. The chambers of revolvers were by this time stepped to accommodate the oversized case, tapering down to ensure a good gas seal on the bullet as it left the case on firing. The cases retained a solid rim, which prevented the cartridge sliding forwards into the chamber, and provided a headspace point. The bullets were still made of lead and without metal jackets, since the low velocities of handgun ammunition – 600–900ft (183–274m) per second – did not cause significant lead fouling in the barrel.

The developments of self-loading pistols in the 1890s followed the introduction of high-pressure smokeless propellants. Self-loaders worked best with rimless pistol rounds which were parallel-sided or bottle-necked, with a recessed rim or extractor groove for an extractor to grip during firing and cycling. Metallic jackets for the bullets were necessary to prevent lead build-up in the barrel. The Hague Convention for the rules of war effectively outlawed the use of exposed lead in service ammunition, even in those of low velocity, and a metal jacket of copper or steel became commonplace in military handgun ammunition. By the beginning of the First World War the principal Western repeating pistol and revolver calibres had been established, and most subsequent "new" calibres were just lengthened and strengthened versions of the same thing. The world's two most popular handgun calibres today, 9mm Luger for pistols and ·38 ins Smith & Wesson Special for revolvers, were both launched in 1902. Only in the second half of this century have any significantly new calibres been developed.

BIRTH OF THE MODERN MAGNUMS

The smokeless propellants of the turn of the century gave ammunition manufacturers the opportunity to develop high velocity ammunition. This was particularly suited to pistols, where the closed breech prevented the gas loss experienced in revolvers. The Mauser 1896 pistol used a high-powered version of Borchardt's 7·65mm cartridge known as 7·63mm Mauser to propel a light 86 grain bullet to 1,410 ft per second (fps), the fastest commercial handgun round available until the ·357 Magnum was introduced for revolvers. In Great Britain in the early 1900s, Hugh Gabbet-Fairfax designed the ill-fated Mars pistol, which fired a 9mm 156 grain bullet at 1,650 fps, developing nearly three times the energy of 9mm Luger or 7·63mm Mauser. The Mars was never adopted for service use due to its complexity, size and recoil, but it demonstrated the power that could now be generated by handgun ammunition using smokeless propellants. High velocities were confined to fairly small bores and light bullets, since pressure drops off very rapidly in large calibres due to the large barrel volume left by the departing bullet. In order to keep up the pressure and attain high velocities, a lot of slow burning propellant is required, which in turn needs a large cartridge case. Too large for butt magazine pistols, which had become the best balanced self-loading pistol layout, it was left to revolver cartridges to make the next advances in velocity and muzzle energy.

MAGNUM REVOLVER CARTRIDGES

■ ·357 MAGNUM

The first modern magnum cartridge, ·357 Magnum, was developed in 1935 by Smith & Wesson and Winchester for S&W's heavy frame revolvers. Basically a ·38 S&W Special

■ The ·38 S&W revolver cartridge (**left**) originated around 1877. The improved ·38 S&W Special (**2nd left**) with smokeless powder was introduced in 1902. This itself was stretched in 1935 to give the ·357 S&W Magnum (**second right**), one of the most popular revolver cartridges in use today. A further lengthening of the case in 1983 gave the ·357 Maximum (**right**), which can generate over 1100 ft lbs of muzzle energy.

■ For many years the most powerful handgun cartridge in the world, the ·44 Magnum has proved to be an excellent cartridge for hunting, silhouette shooting and personal defence.

case lengthened by ·135 ins to prevent it being chambered in ·38 revolvers, the ·357 Magnum cartridge produced three times the muzzle energy of the ·38 Special and is now the most popular high velocity revolver round in the world. Originally loaded to push a 158 grain bullet out of an 8¾ ins revolver barrel at over 1,500 fps, the ·357 Magnum has now been backed off in pressure and today factory loadings give 1,200–1,300 fps with a 158 grain bullet, and 1,450 fps with a lighter 125 grain bullet.

■ ·44 REMINGTON MAGNUM

Twenty years later, Smith & Wesson and Remington produced the ·44 Magnum, egged on by Elmer Keith, a bullet designer, hunter and pistol shooter who had developed a number of high velocity loadings for ·44 Special and ·45 Colt. Until recently, this was the most powerful handgun cartridge in the world and owes a lot of its notoriety to the cinema actor Clint Eastwood, who in several films of the 1970s and 80s portrayed a fictional San Francisco detective who preferred dealing with low life with the phenomenal stopping power of the .44 Magnum over his issue ·357 Magnum. Like the ·357 Magnum before it, the ·44 Magnum was based on an existing case, the ·44 Special; like the ·38 Special, the ·44 Special was lengthened so that the high pressure round could not be inadvertently used in revolvers made for the low pressure cartridge. The ·44 Special itself had grown out of the ·44 Russian, when bulky, smokeless powders were first used.

▪ ·41 REMINGTON MAGNUM

The recoil and blast of the ·44 Magnum was difficult for inexperienced shooters to control, and in 1967 Smith & Wesson introduced a totally new cartridge designed to fill the gap between the ·357 and ·44 Magnums. The ·41 Magnum was conceived as the ultimate law enforcement calibre, but it was not widely adopted; it could only be fired in a heavy, large frame revolver, and the factory ammunition loadings still had considerable recoil, more than many policemen and women would tolerate. The impressive ballistics and accuracy of the round caught the attention of a few American shooters, who successfully used it for handgun hunting. Today Smith & Wesson and Ruger still produce double-action revolvers chambered for ·41 Magnum, but their sales are not for law enforcement but to sportsmen.

▪ ·32 H&R MAGNUM

Since the Magnum tag seemed to enhance sales of guns and ammunition, in 1984 the Federal Cartridge Company introduced the ·32 Harrington & Richardson Magnum for the now defunct New England gunmakers Harrington & Richardson. Like the ·357 and ·44 Magnums, the ·32 H&R Magnum was based on the existing ·32 Smith & Wesson Long case, lengthened by ·155 ins. Unlike the other Magnums, however, the ·32 was loaded to fairly low pressures, comparable with those of the old ·38 Special.

▪ ·357 REMINGTON MAXIMUM

In the search for a super Magnum revolver cartridge, the ·357 Magnum was stretched by ·3 ins, and the ·357 Remington Maximum was introduced in 1983. Ruger and Dan Wesson produced revolvers chambered for the new calibre, but problems of gas-cutting of the frame in front of the cylinder, and of rapid barrel wear have caused many people to feel that at 1,825 fps with a 158 grain bullet, the safe pressure and velocity limit for a repeating handgun was being exceeded by the ·357 Maximum. The round has been eagerly adopted by single shot pistol manufacturers, however, who have no such gas-cutting problems.

▪ ·454 CASULL

The title of "the most powerful production revolver cartridge in the world" now belongs to the ·454 Casull. This was developed from the ·45 Colt cartridge which had been introduced in the 1873 Peacemaker, and, like the ·32, ·357, and ·44 Magnums, uses a longer and far stronger case than its parent. The ·454 Casull was originally named the ·454 Magnum Revolver by Dick Casull and Jack Fullmer, its inventors in 1957. However, the Magnum designation seems to gain popularity for the wrong reasons these days, and now that five shot ·454 Casull single action revolvers

▪ *The most powerful production revolver cartridge now made is the ·454 Casull which can develop twice the energy of ·44 Magnum when fired from the Freedom Arms Casull.*

▪ *Left The ·41 Magnum was an attempt to produce the "ideal" police revolver cartridge in 1964. The recoil was still too powerful for some officers, but ·41 Magnum has been eagerly accepted by handgun hunters as a good hunting round without the blast of ·44 Magnum.*

are being made for the cartridge by Freedom Arms Inc, the production cartridge carries the designer's name instead. Factory ammunition pushes a 260 grain bullet to 1,720 feet per second giving 1,700ft.lbs of muzzle energy, nearly twice that of a factory loaded ·44 Magnum, and 40 times that of the first rimfire ·22s.

■ ·45–70 GOVERNMENT

Big bore single action revolvers are now being chambered for ·45–70 Government, an old parallel-sided black powder rifle cartridge used by the US military from 1873 to 1892. While the case is even larger than that of the Casull, it was originally designed for black powder propellant and is not strong enough for Magnum pressures approaching those of the Casull. The ·45–70 is not officially classed as a handgun cartridge.

■ *The vintage black powder rifle cartridge, the ·45–70 Gov't (**centre**) is now being chambered in big bore single action revolvers. Either side stand the ·357 Magnum and ·44 Magnum.*

■ ·22 REMINGTON JET AND ·256 WINCHESTER MAGNUM

With an aim to developing better Magnum revolver cartridges, both Remington and Winchester played with bottle-necked rounds in 1960–1961 based on the ·357 Magnum case. Remington necked down the case to produce the ·22 Remington Jet, firing a ·223 ins 40 grain bullet to 2,460 fps from an 8½ ins Smith & Wesson barrel. Winchester made the ·256 Winchester Magnum handgun cartridge, which fired a 60 grain bullet at 2,200 fps that could penetrate a ¼ ins (6mm) steel plate, but no handgun manufacturer produced a revolver chambered for it. While the fast, light bullet gave high energies with minimal recoil, the tapered, bottle-necked case tended to back out of the cylinder on firing, locking up the whole gun. Both cartridges are still occasionally chambered in single shot pistols, but no longer in revolvers.

THE SUPERMAGS: FUTURE DEVELOPMENTS

For the sport of metal silhouette shooting in the US there is a need for high energy revolver calibres to knock down extreme range targets, with ·44 Magnum and ·357 Maximum only just up to the job. The revolver manufacturers Dan Wesson have been working with silhouette shooter Elgin Gates to produce even longer versions of ·357 and ·44 calibres known as the Super Magnums or Supermags using a cartridge case length of 1·610 inches, 25% longer than the parent Magnums. At present these calibres are not loaded commercially, since the users of them will be handloaders, who tailor the ammunition to suit the handgun it is used in.

MAGNUM PISTOL AMMUNITION

■ 9mm MAUSER

It was only natural that attempts would be made to develop "Magnum" ammunition for self-loading pistols, since they would hold more cartridges than the five or six in a centre-fire revolver, giving a theoretical firepower advantage. One of the earliest attempts was by Mauser, who launched the 9mm Mauser as a higher powered version of the 7·63mm Model 1896. Since only their pistols were chambered for 9mm Mauser, and they were expensive, the cartridge did not catch on and was discontinued in 1914.

■ ·38 SUPER

In 1929 Colt beefed up the Government pistol and chambered it for ·38 Super Automatic, dimensionally identical to their 1900 designed ·38 Auto Colt round, but loaded to a higher pressure and giving substantially improved velocities. Despite using a powerful cartridge, the pistols were less accurate than many of their competitors since the Colt headspaced on the semi-rim of the case. ·38 Super ammunition was given a new lease of life in the 1970s when after-market barrels became available; these improved the accuracy by headspacing on the case mouth, as with the 9mm Luger and ·45 ACP. In the 1980s, the cartridge attracted the interest of IPSC competition shooters who built Colt-type pistols for it using custom-made barrels with recoil reducing compensators fitted to them. Reloaded ·38 Super has become a very popular cartridge for top grade shooters.

■ ·357 & ·44 AUTO MAG

In 1970–1971, the Auto Mag pistol was made and chambered for two new cartridges, ·357 Auto Mag and ·44 Auto Mag, made by cutting down ·308 Win or ·30–06 rifle cases. The ·44 left the case almost parallel-sided, while the ·357 necked the case down to make a bottlenecked-type round which gives no problems in self-loaders. Velocity and energy was impressive from both rounds, but only one manufacturer eventually made new brass cases, and there was only the one rather unreliable make of pistol which is no longer produced. Like the 9mm Mauser, the Auto Mags have all but disappeared.

9mm & ·45 WINCHESTER MAGNUM

1979 saw the introduction of two similarly high-powered rounds, 9mm Winchester Magnum and ·45 Winchester Magnum, made by Winchester for the Wildey gas-operated self-loading pistol. Both cartridges were new designs, but followed the revolver magnum tradition of being based on existing cases lengthened to prevent them being used in older pistols. The gas operation of the Wildey pistol also tamed the recoil. LAR Manufacturing subsequently produced an oversized pistol, based on the 1911 Colt, to chamber the two rounds. ·45 Win Mag is comparable in velocity and energy to the ·44 Magnum revolver round, and the 9mm Win Mag similar to the ·357 Magnum.

·451 DETONICS MAGNUM

In 1983, Detonics shortened the ·45 Winchester Magnum case to make a slightly improved version of the ·45 ACP ammunition used in their normal frame Colt 1911-type pistols. ·451 Detonics Magnum takes the middle ground between ·45 ACP and ·45 Win Mag, pushing a 200 grain bullet to around 1,250 fps/700 ft.lbs energy, heavy but controllable.

10mm AUTO

An intermediate high performance calibre between ·38 and ·44 has often been promoted as the "ideal" for law enforcement and personal defence, with Smith & Wesson's ·41 Mag revolver being one attempt to popularize the idea. Inspired by Col. Jeff Cooper, a combat shooting and self defence instructor, Dornaus & Dixon Enterprises of California manufactured a pistol in 1983 based on the tough Czechoslovakian CZ75 9mm Luger self-loader, and called it the Bren 10. Norma of Sweden produced the all-new ammunition it chambered, 10mm Auto (·40 inch calibre). Unfortunately the Bren 10 pistol manufacturers ceased trading, leaving Norma with a vast stockpile of ammunition. At the end of the 1980s, other pistol manufacturers awoke to the potential of 10mm Auto, and Colt launched their Delta Elite chambered for it. The 10mm Auto compares well to the ·41 Magnum, with similar energy and ballistics but a short enough case to allow the use of a high capacity staggered magazine in a pistol.

·41 ACTION EXPRESS

The problem with 10mm, however, is that considerable retooling is required to modify the slides and barrels of

■ Another attempt at producing the "ideal" combat cartridge was the 10mm Auto pistol round designed for the ill-fated Bren Ten.

Illustrated is the Colt Delta Elite, a derivative of the Colt 1911 which is chambered for 10mm Auto.

existing design pistols to chamber it. Unlike the 9mm/·357/·44/·45 Magnums, a totally new 10mm bullet is needed too. The American pistol importers Action Arms then had a brainwave: they designed a ·41 ins auto pistol cartridge which would use existing ·41 bullets, but would use the same rim size as 9mm Luger. The only modification to a pistol design would be a barrel with a bigger bore and chamber, and possibly slightly altered magazines. Working with a Swiss copy of the CZ75, the ITM AT 84, a pistol was soon developed and Israel Military Industries produced ammunition for them known as ·41 Action Express. This punched a 200 grain bullet to 1,120 fps velocity with an acceptable level of recoil. The race is now on to see whether 10mm Auto or ·41 AE can become established as the new ideal combat pistol round.

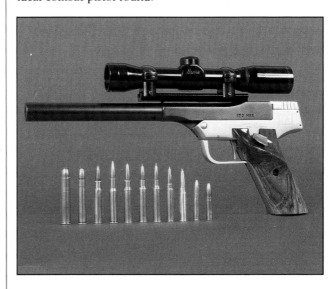

■ Single shot pistols have few constraints on the type of

ammunition they can use and many are chambered for rifle cartridges.

SINGLE SHOT PISTOL AMMUNITION

Single shot pistols do not have any of the problems of ammunition length, gas leakage or flame cutting that have plagued designers of revolvers and self-loaders. The distinction between a pistol and a rifle round is now blurred by the use of rifle ammunition in single shot pistols designed for hunting and metallic silhouette target shooting. Most of the popular "one shooters" are available in all calibres from ·22 Long Rifle up to ·35 Remington and ·308 WCF/7·62 × 51mm.

■ JDJ WILDCATS

J. D. Jones of SSK Industries has produced a new range of "wildcat" calibres, with the suffix "JDJ", for use in his replacement barrels for the single shot Thompson Center Contender pistol, based on the ·225 Winchester and ·444 Marlin rifle cartridge cases. Wildcat is the expression used for ammunition which is not sold by proprietary manufacturers, but is made by individuals using existing cases re-

formed to suit their requirements. After a number of years, some wildcats are accepted as production calibres in their own right, and new brass and ammunition becomes available.

■ ·221 REMINGTON FIREBALL

In 1963, Remington Arms introduced their XP-100 single shot bolt action pistol which was based on a shortened rifle action. The pistol was chambered for ·221 Remington Fireball, a new pistol calibre based on the ·222 Remington rifle cartridge. The ·221 Fireball produces the highest velocity of any of the nominal handgun cartridges, the factory load reaching 2,650 fps with a 50 grain bullet.

DUAL PURPOSE CARTRIDGES

The traditional centrefire revolver round is parallel-sided with a rim at the primer end to prevent the case slipping into the chamber. A self-loading pistol round can be parallel (·38 Super), tapered (9mm Luger) or bottlenecked (7·63mm Mauser), and is usually rimless or semi-rimmed with an extractor groove. Over the years, however, some self-loading pistols have been made to fire five or six revolver cartridges, usually for target use, since the revolver cartridge's rimmed case causes stacking problems if too many are pushed into a pistol's magazine. Target pistols are available in the revolver calibres ·22 Short, ·22 Long Rifle, ·32 S&W Long (firing a flush-seated wadcutter bullet) and ·38 Special (also firing a flush-seated wadcutter bullet). Recently Coonan Arms, Inc. began manufacturing an elegant, stainless steel Colt 1911–type delayed blowback pistol which fires the revolver ·357 Magnum, and Israel Military Industries produce a massive gas-operated self-loader in versions chambered for both ·357 Magnum and ·44 Magnum revolver cartridges.

■ ·45 AUTO RIM

There have also been attempts to use rimless pistol ammunition in revolvers by using "half moon" clips to prevent the cartridges sliding into the chamber. This was very popular during the First World War, with the ·45 ACP cartridge used in revolvers with modified cylinders. In 1920, the Peters Cartridge Company produced a thick rimmed ·45 cartridge, the ·45 Auto Rim, which could be used in place of ·45 ACP and clips. For a brief period, Smith & Wesson made the 547 K frame revolver for export which used tapered 9mm Luger ammunition without the need for

■ *Rimless ·45 ACP pistol ammunition held in "half moon" or "full moon" clips can be used in appropriate revolvers.*

extra clips. Federal have now made a rimmed 9mm revolver round, but this is a new cartridge and is not just thick rimmed 9mm Luger.

PISTOL AND REVOLVER AMMUNITION IN PRODUCTION TODAY

Many of the old pistol and revolver cartridges have disappeared due to their ineffectiveness and lack of demand,

■ *Opposite One of the few self-loading pistols to successfully use a rimmed revolver cartridge is the stainless steel Coonan ·357 Magnum Automatic.*

■ *The same basic handgun – an S&W Model 10 – and the same basic ammunition – ·38 Special – with two totally different uses. The customized heavy barrelled "PPC" revolver based on the Model 10 (**right**) uses soft recoiling wadcutter ammunition for target shooting. For law enforcement, the 2 in Snubby is loaded with +P hollowpoints.*

although some are still available even though they were first designed over 100 years ago. A few calibres are still made with black powder propellant, even though that was superseded by the cleaner, less corrosive smokeless powders at the turn of the century. The introduction of non-mercuric lead styphnate primers in the 1920s made ammunition totally non-corrosive, but even after the widespread adoption of non-corrosive primers by Western manufacturers by the late 1950s, some European and Eastern Bloc factories are still using corrosive mercury fulminate and potassium chlorate for ignition in handgun ammunition.

The 9mm Luger, also known as 9mm Parabellum and 9 × 19mm, has become the standard pistol round of most Western armies, with a similar but shorter round, 9 × 18mm Makarov, being used in the Eastern Bloc. 9mm Luger is also set to topple ·38 Special and ·357 Magnum from their positions as first choice for domestic law enforcement in the United States and Great Britain now that police hostility to self-loaders is decreasing. ·38 Special and ·357 Magnum will always be very popular with civilians for defence and sport, since they have minimal recoil and are economical to reload for practice. The smaller pistol calibres, ·380/9mmK, ·32 Auto/7·65mm, and ·25 Auto/6·35mm, are also surprisingly popular for personal defence, despite being inefficient manstoppers. Until recently, ·32 Auto was a common European law enforcement calibre and is still used by some officers for personal and back-up pistols.

For pure, precision target pistol shooting, the ·22 rimfire rounds, ·22 Short and ·22 Long Rifle, are the only two used in smallbore events. For international centrefire disciplines ·32 Smith & Wesson Long and ·38 Smith & Wesson Special both dominate, and both are used with special hollow-based wadcutter target bullets which give exceptional accuracy at low velocities with minimal recoil.

■ *Aluminium cartridge cases are now used for full power training ammunition. Plastic cases have been introduced for the same purpose loaded with conventional bullets and propellants. Plastic cases with plastic bullets are also used for training in house clearance scenarios or "man v man" exercises.*

The ·45 ACP was finally shelved in favour of 9mm Luger by the US Army in 1985 after more than 70 years in their principal sidearms, the Colt 1911 and 1911 A1 pistols. The calibre is still very popular with civilians for personal defence because of its good stopping power and moderate recoil, and it still just about holds its own against ·38 Super as the top round for IPSC combat target pistol shooting while the impact of the new 10mm and ·41 AE calibres on the sport is assessed.

The big bore Magnum ·41/·44/·45 calibres are most popular for hunting and metallic silhouette target shooting, where sufficient accuracy and energy has to be retained by the bullet to kill an animal up to 100 yards (91·5m) or knock down a heavy steel plate at 250 yards (228m). The softer shooting ·44 Special is also an excellent defence calibre.

NOMENCLATURE

The names and sizes given to handgun ammunition frequently causes confusion. Calibres of apparently different sizes will often use the same bullet (e.g. ·38 Special and ·357 Magnum). On occasion, two dimensionally identical rounds have been given different calibre designations because of different pressure ratings (e.g. 7·65mm Borchardt and 7·63mm Mauser). The modern ·44s are not really ·44 inches in bore at all and use a smaller ·429 ins bullet! In Europe, some (but not all) calibres are described by the metric size rather than an Imperial designation (e.g. ·32 Automatic and 7·65mm Browning).

Part of the size problem began during the transition from externally to internally lubricated bullets. The old ·44 American cartridge used a heeled and externally lubricated ·434 ins bullet and a case base diameter of ·440 ins. When this was changed to ·44 Russian, the new calibre used an internally lubricated ·429 ins bullet and a case base diameter of ·457 ins. The sizing error has been perpetuated to this day in the ·44 Magnum, partly because the ·44 calibre reeks of history – it was the calibre of the percussion revolvers used to fight the American Civil War – and partly because it rolls off the tongue better. "Forty-four" sounds smoother than "point four-two-nine"! In more recent times, the actual bore size is used to denote the calibre. ·357 Magnum actually is ·357 ins; ·41 Magnum is correct, as is 10mm Auto and ·454 Casull.

A few calibres have interchangeable metric and Imperial sizes; ·25 Auto is the same as 6·35mm Browning, ·32 Auto is 7·65mm Browning, and ·380 Auto is 9mm Browning Short – which is often also called 9mm Kurz or 9mmK.

The names of other calibres are frequently shortened. ·45 Automatic Colt Pistol is usually known as ·45 ACP. Manufacturers' names are usually shortened or dropped if there is

■ *Recently retired by the US Military after 70 years service, the ·45 ACP cartridge is still popular with IPSC target shooters where it competes against handloaded ·38 Super in the "Major" Calibre power band.*

not likely to be confusion with other similar calibres. ·38 Smith & Wesson Special is normally abbreviated to ·38 Spl, and ·44 Remington Magnum to ·44 Magnum or ·44 Mag. However ·38 Smith & Wesson and ·32 Smith & Wesson Long always retain the Smith & Wesson tag, usually shortened to S&W, to differentiate them from the obsolete ·38 Short Colt and ·32 Long Colt.

9mm Luger has been called by a variety of names, 9mm Parabellum being the most common alternative, and also 9 × 19mm – the "19" describing the case length. The correct designation recently agreed internationally is 9mm Luger, which I usually annotate as 9mmLu.

A recent addition to the range of 9mm calibres has been 9 × 21mm which has similar power to 9mm Luger. It has been developed because some European countries do not permit civilians to possess handguns chambered for military calibres. It is quite simple for manufacturers to ream the chambers of 9mm Luger pistols by an extra 2mm, and therefore sell the handguns as 9 × 21mm calibre.

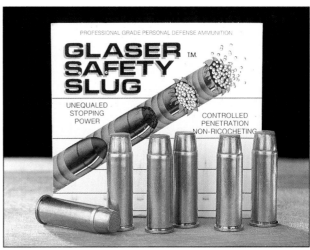

■ *The Glaser Safety Slug is one of a new breed of exotic handgun ammunition. The Glaser "bullet" is actually a thin copper cup filled with fine lead shot in liquid teflon and sealed with a plastic plug. On impact the slug "dumps" all its energy with impressive knockdown power. If the target is missed, the slug will not ricochet but will splash against the first hard object it meets.*

CURRENT HANDGUN CALIBRES PRODUCED TODAY

Calibre	Revolver/Pistol/Single shot pistol	Use: Sport/Defence/Military/Law Enf.	Bullet diameter inches	Weight range grains	Velocity range feet per second
RIMFIRE					
·22 Long RF	R&P	S	·224	29	1055
·22 Long Rifle RF	R&P	S	·224	40	1000–1150
·22 Short RF	R&P	S	·224	29	865
·22 Winchester Magnum Rimfire	R&P	S	·224	40	1550
CENTREFIRE					
5·45mm Russian	P	M	·22	40 est	1400 est
·22 Rem Jet	R&SSP	S	·223	40	2460
·221 Rem Fireball	SSP	S	·224	50	2650
·25 Auto/6·35mmBr	P	D	·251	50	810
·256 Win Magnum	R&SSP	S	·257	60	2200
7·62 × 17mm Chinese	P	M	·307	60	1050
7·62mm Nagent	R	S	·295	108	725
7·62mm Tokarev	P	M	·307	87	1390
7·63mm Mauser	P	D	·308	86	1410
7·65mm Luger	P	D	·308	93	1220
·32 Auto/7·65mmBr	P	D/L	·309	60–71	905–970
·32 H&R Magnum	R	S/D	·312	85–95	1030–1100
·32 S&W Long	R&P	S/D	·312	92	780
8mm Nambu	P	M	·320	102	960
9×21mm	P	S/D	·355	110–125	1000–1200
9mm Federal Rev	R	L/D	·355	115	1280
9mm Largo	P	M/L	·355	125	1120
9mm Luger/9mm Para/9×19mm	P	M/L/D/S	·355	90–158	900–1230
9mm Makarov	P	M	·363	94	1115
9mm Ultra/9×18mm	P	D/L	·355	94–100	1060
9mm Win Magnum	P	S/D	·355	115	1475
·357 Win Magnum	R&P	S/D/L	·357	110–158	1235–1450
·357 Rem Maximum	R	S	·357	158–180	1550–1825
·38 S&W	R	S/D	·359	145–200	630–730
·38 S&W Spl	R&P	S/D/L	·357	110–200	730–1020
·380 Auto/9mmK	P	S/D/L	·356	85–95	955–1000
·38 Auto	P	D	·358	130	1040
·38 Super Auto	P	S/D	·358	115–130	1275–1300
10mm Auto	P	S/D	·400	200	1250
·41 Action Express	P	S/D	·410	170–200	1120–1220
·41 Rem Magnum	R	S/D/L	·410	210	1150–1500
·44 S&W Spl	R	S/D	·429	246	755
·44 Rem Magnum	R&P	S/D/L	·429	240	1350
·45 ACP	R&P	M/L/D/S	·452	185–230	755–1000
·45 Auto Rim	R	D	·452	230	805
·45 Colt	R	S/D	·454	255	855
·45 Win Magnum	P	S/D	·452	230	1400
·451 Detonics Mag	P	S/D	·451	185–200	1280–1350
·454 Casull	R	S	·454	225–300	1350–1740

■ **BULLET SIZES** are nominal, jacketed bullets used in handgun ammunition are usually made to the nominal size. Lead bullets are often made ·001–·002 inches larger in diameter.

■ **AMMUNITION** is also still manufactured for revolvers chambering the following obsolete cartridges:
·32 Smith & Wesson, ·32 Short Colt, ·32 Long Colt, ·38 Smith & Wesson, ·38 Short Colt, ·450 Revolver, ·455 Webley MkII

■ *Hollowpoint bullets and ammunition are available in most handgun calibres from ·22 to ·45 for sport or survival. In theory the hollow nose mushrooms on impact, imparting most of the energy into the target. In practice, high velocities are needed for significant and effective expansion.*

■ *Top* *The most popular military handgun cartridge in the world is 9mm Luger which is also used in machine pistols and sub machine guns. 9mm is also becoming a favourite of Police and law enforcement agencies.*

■ *Left* *"Wildcat" cartridges like ·309 JDJ and ·375 JDJ (**1st & 2nd left**) are used for handgun hunting in addition to ·45–70 Gov't, 7mm/08 and 50–70. A "tiny" ·44 Magnum stands on the far right.*

CURRENT HANDGUN CALIBRES PRODUCED TODAY: THE VELOCITY LEAGUE IN FEET PER SECOND

The velocities are quoted from manufacturers specification sheets. Substantially higher velocities can be achieved by careful handloading. The author has reached 2000 fps with a 200 grain ·44 Magnum from a 14" barrel, the same load giving 1725 fps from a 7½" barrel.

Calibre	500	1000	1500	2000	2500	
·221 Rem Fireball						2650
·22 Rem Jet						2460
·256 Win Magnum						2200
·357 Rem Maximum					1825	
·454 Cassull					1740	
·22 WMR				1550		
·41 Rem Magnum				1500		
9mm Win Magnum				1475		
·357 Win Magnum				1450		
7·63mm Mauser				1410		
·45 Win Magnum				1400		
5·45mm Russian				1400 (estimated)		
7·62mm Tokarev				1390		
·451 Detonics Mag				1350		
·44 Rem Magnum				1350		
·38 Super Auto			1300			
9mm Federal Rev			1280			
10mm Auto			1250			
9mm Luger			1230			
7·65mm Luger			1220			
·41 Action Express			1220			
9 × 21mm			1200			
·22 Long Rifle RF			1150			
9mm Largo			1120			
9mm Makarov			1115			
·32 H&R Magnum			1100			
9mm Ultra/9 × 18mm		1060				
·22 Long RF		1055				
7·62×17mm Chinese		1050				
·38 Auto		1040				
·38 S&W Spl		1020				
·380 Auto/9mmK		1000				
·45 ACP		1000				
·32 Auto/7·65mmBr		970				
8mm Nambu		960				
·22 Short RF		865				
·45 Colt		855				
·25 Auto/6·35mmBr		810				
·45 Auto Rim		805				
·32 S&W Long		780				
·44 S&W Spl		755				
·38 S&W		730				
7·62mm Nagent		725				

CURRENT HANDGUN CALIBRES PRODUCED TODAY:
THE POWER LEAGUE – MUZZLE ENERGY IN FT. LBS

Muzzle energy in foot-lbs is calculated from the square of the bullets velocity multiplied by its weight in pounds, divided by twice the acceleration due to gravity. Light bullets at high velocities have higher energies than slower heavier bullets from the same gun.

The muzzle energy calculation puts service 9mm Luger ammunition on a par with service ·45 ACP at 330 ft. lbs. The energy is not the only factor in a bullet's 'stopping power' however. The cross sectional area and the bullet design also affect stopping power. Two of the most effective and controllable rounds are ·357 Magnum 125 grain jacketed hollow points travelling at 1450 fps which have substantial 'shock power', and 230 grain round nosed ·45 ACP bullets travelling at 800 fps which have a heavy 'knockdown' power.

Calibre	0	100	250	500	750	1000	1250	1500	
·454 Casull									1700
·357 Rem Maximum							1170		
·41 Rem Magnum							1050		
·44 Rem Magnum							1010		
·45 Win Magnum							1000		
·221 Rem Fireball					780				
·451 Detonics Mag					750				
10mm Auto					695				
·256 Win Magnum					650				
·41 Action Express				560					
9mm Win Magnum				555					
·22 Rem Jet				540					
·357 Win Magnum				535					
·38 Super Auto				470					
9mm Federal Rev				420					
·45 Colt				415					
·45 ACP				410					
7·63mm Mauser				380					
7·62mm Tokarev				375					
9mm Largo				350					
9 × 21mm				345					
9mm Luger				345					
·45 Auto Rim				330					
·38 Auto				310					
·44 S&W Spl				310					
7·65mm Luger				305					
9mm Makarov			260						
9mm Ultra/9 × 18mm			250						
·38 S&W Spl			250						
·32 H&R Magnum			225						
·22 WMR			215						
8mm Nambu			210						
·380 Auto/9mmK			195						
·38 S&W		175							
5·45mm Russian		175							
7·62 × 17mm Chinese		140							
7·62mm Nagent		125							
·32 S&W Long		125							
·22 Long Rifle RF		120							
·32 Auto/7·65mmBr		110							
·25 Auto/6·35mmBr	75								
·22 Long RF	70								
·22 Short RF	50								

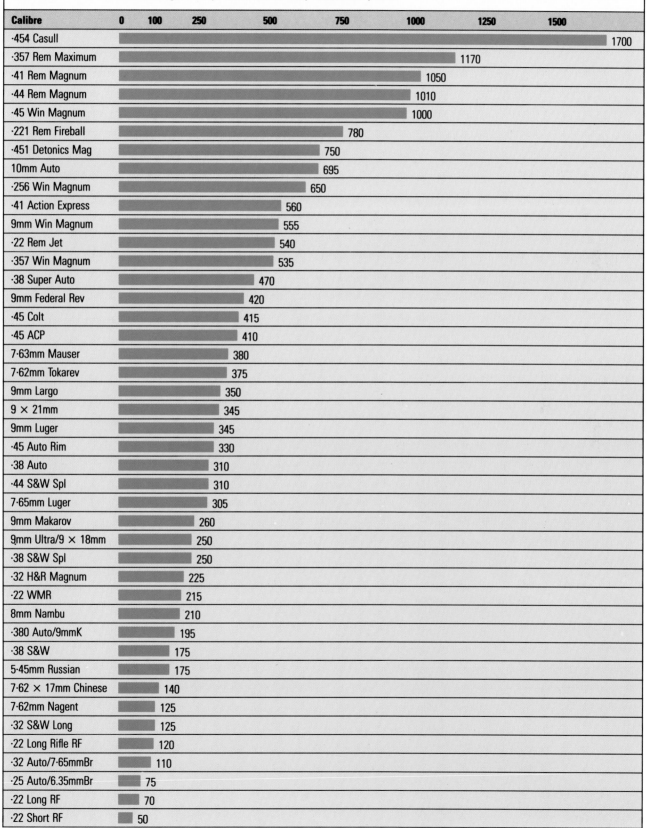

HANDGUN MANUFACTURERS

There has not been a major global military conflict for over 40 years, but since 1945 several parts of the world have been fighting one another with firearms in minor skirmishes or "police actions". With the advent of the machine pistol and assault rifle, handguns have generally remained a military weapon of last resort for purely personal defence, and handgun manufacture in many countries is restricted to the requirements for internal policing and supplying basic military demands. It has also proved cheaper and more efficient for some countries to purchase proven handguns from abroad, or to manufacture them under licence, than to engage in outright new design and production. A degree of natural conservatism among arms procurement officers has led to the dependence of many on a small selection of large manufacturers to supply their requirements, either directly or under licence by domestic engineering companies.

In the West, this has meant the growth of a few handgun manufacturers who dominate military and police sales. Their principal products are also purchased by civilians for sport and defence because of the endorsement given by military contracts. In some Western countries, however, smaller arms manufacturers have developed, supplying inexpensive handguns to civilians for defence, or highly specialized sporting pistols for recreational target shooting and hunting.

The range of handguns manufactured in the Communist East is limited; while the bulk are service weapons, a few are made for export or for sporting use.

HANDGUN MANUFACTURERS IN THE US

Without doubt, the greatest number of manufacturers is concentrated in the United States, and they make up half of the 120 listed in the Appendix at the back of this book. In the 13 years 1973–1985, the American arms producers made almost 26 million handguns, two thirds of which were revolvers, **in addition to those made for the US Armed Forces.** American handgun manufacture reached a peak in 1981, when over 2½ million were made for police and civilian sales, nearly 10 times the output of a low in 1954. Since 1981, production has dropped as the market contracted, causing the closure of the then fourth largest US manufacturer, Harrington & Richardson, and the collapse of the established and innovative Iver Johnson Company.

■ America's largest handgun manufacturer, Smith & Wesson have not changed their basic revolver design for 80 years. Their "new" ·44 Magnum, the Classic Hunter, still has cylinder notches machined over the chambers, weakening a critical stress point.

■ *Ruger's rugged revolvers have built up an excellent reputation for strength and reliability. Illustrated are the Redhawk ·44 Mag models in blue and stainless finish.*

The number of handguns exported also reached a peak in 1981, but this only accounted for 13% of the total US production in that year. The bulk of the exports in 1981 were revolvers, nearly a third of a million compared with a little over 25,000 pistols, a ratio which fairly reflected the manufacturing trend.

With increasing acceptance of the self-loading pistol by police forces, the ratio of pistols to revolvers made has steadily increased from 21% of the US total in 1974 to 46% in 1985. Despite this, 40% of all the US handguns made from 1973–85 were revolvers in the calibres ·38 and ·357. The total includes slightly more ·38s, but the trend since 1978 has been for more ·357s to be made annually, reaching a peak in 1981 of 524,000 units.

Out of the 60-odd manufacturing companies in the US, almost 60% of American handguns are made by the "Big Three" – Colt, Ruger, and Smith & Wesson. In the years 1973–86, Smith & Wesson made more handguns at their Springfield, Massachusetts factory than the other two put together.

■ SMITH & WESSON

Smith & Wesson's strength is in the double action revolver, where four basic frame sizes are used to produce a range of 29 models in carbon and stainless steel. The variations on each model of barrel length and type, finish, and grip style gives a choice of almost 100 revolvers in seven revolver cal-

ibres from ·22 Long Rifle to ·45 Colt. The pistol range is comparatively small, with only 11 models in four calibres – ·22 LR, 9mm Luger, ·38 Spl-WC and ·45 ACP. Sadly, Smith & Wesson has not improved the basic design of its revolvers for 80 years, and while a well-tuned S&W trigger is a joy to shoot, the anachronistic practice of machining the cylinder notches over the chambers on the weakest part of the cylinder limits their potential with hand-loaded Magnum ammunition. Smith & Wesson produced the original ·357 Magnum and ·44 Magnum revolvers on its largest "N" frame, and ·357 Magnum is now chambered in the medium "K" and "L" frames.

Although Smith & Wesson has a significant place in American history and produces a large number of domestic American handguns, the ownership of the company moved to Great Britain in 1987 when F. H. Tomkins purchased the business from Lear-Siegler Holdings for US$112.5 million. The new owners intend to rationalize the company, putting more emphasis on the 9mm Luger calibre pistol range, so that Smith & Wesson will be better placed to tender for military and police self-loading pistol contracts.

■ RUGER

Sturm, Ruger & Co, Inc. of Southport, Connecticut, US, is the second largest American producer of handguns, and, like Smith & Wesson, has built up a good reputation with its revolvers. Ruger also produces rifles and shotguns, and

■ *Colt have recently rationalized their product range to two double action revolvers and a handful of old design self-loaders. Their Custom Gun department produces special order single action Peacemakers and commemoratives like this Sheriff's model display.*

has recently launched its first 9mm Luger pistol, the P85. Compared to Smith & Wesson and Colt, Ruger is the new boy, having started business in 1949, 100 years after the others. The key to Ruger's success has been its skill at building on the success of others; it has avoided wasting time developing radical products which would have a long acceptance time before achieving high volume sales. Once a design has been finalized, it is made in high volume with the most modern methods, giving low-priced handguns which represent good value for money. None of Ruger's products are copies, but it frequently takes well-proven, basic features and improve them for reasons of reliability and safety. The single action Blackhawks and Single-Sixes are perhaps the best example. Modelled on the popular 1873 Colt Peacemaker, Ruger have added a modern transfer bar safety (to allow the gun to be carried hammer down on a loaded chamber), a floating firing pin and a coil mainspring. The Blackhawk is tough enough to stand the pressures of modern Magnum ammunition, and is often used as the basis for special big bore five shooters used by South African handgun hunters like Ross Seyfried, with his ·50 and ·475 calibre Linebaugh conversions.

Ruger produces the only "modern" muzzle-loading black powder revolver made today, the ·44 ins Old Army. Outwardly similar in appearance to the antique cap and ball percussion revolvers which are widely copied at the Italian replica factories, the Old Army has adjustable target-type sights, a modern single action trigger mechanism, and an integral baffle on the cylinder to prevent too rapid a build-up of fouling on the cylinder spindle. The Old Army has proved to be too good to compete on equal terms with the antique and replica revolvers used for international muzzle-loading target shooting, and is banned from such events. They are used by club level shooters for target practice and "pistol" matches, and by US citizens as a sidearm when hunting with black powder rifles.

Ruger's double action revolvers win no contests for beauty or smoothness of trigger pull, but they are favoured by many police departments as training and service pistols as they have a very low failure rate under heavy use compared with other manufacturer's products. The acceptance of the medium frame Service-Six, Speed-Six and large frame Redhawk revolvers has prompted Ruger into producing a "system" revolver, the GP100, incorporating all the others' best features.

In addition to the new P85 pistol, Ruger manufactures a well-made, low priced ·22 LR pistol for casual target shooting and as a trail gun. The current model is the Mark II and some fully silenced versions are alleged to be favoured by covert security teams for assassinations.

■ COLT

One of the oldest names in American repeating handguns, Colt, is still in business in Hartford, Connecticut, US – but only just. Now the third largest American handgun manufacturer, Colt recently suffered a year-long strike of its production workers which hit output and quality. Many of the older revolver products, such as the Diamondback, Trooper,

Detective Special and Agent, have been dropped, leaving just two double action revolvers, the Python and the King Cobra, both in ·357 Magnum. The Python is a high priced, high quality target revolver, claimed by Colt to be the finest production revolver in the world – which will no doubt be disputed by a number of European target revolver manufacturers. The Cobra is a low priced revolver produced for the police and personal defence.

Colt's self-loading pistol range is based on the old 1911A1 design with only the smaller ·380 Auto Mustangs differing in any degree to the vintage military service pistol. The large "O" frame pistols are available in 9mm Luger, ·38 Super and ·45 ACP. A slightly modified and stronger Colt 1911-type pistol, the Delta Elite in the new 10mm Auto calibre, was launched in 1987. When the armies of the world seem to want high capacity double action self-loading pistols, Colt resolutely perseveres with its fine, old, low magazine capacity, single action pistols.

One of Colt's most famous revolvers, the 1873 Single Action Army Model (the Peacemaker) is still available in ·44–40 and ·45 Colt through Colt's custom shop, which specializes in low volume, high priced commemorative handguns.

■ CHARTER ARMS AND DAN WESSON

Despite the saturation of the American market by the Big Three, there is still room for smaller companies in the personal defence and sporting fields. Charter Arms of Stratford, Connecticut, US, manufactures a small range of lightweight defence revolvers in calibres from ·22 LR to ·44 Special. Dan Wesson Arms of Monson, Massachusetts, engineers a range of very accurate, interchangeable barrel revolvers favoured by many long range steel silhouette shooters.

■ *Dan Wesson's revolvers are becoming favourites of silhouette shooters in the US. Dan Wesson also chamber their revolvers for the "Supermag" range of wildcat cartridges based on rifle cases.*

■ BERETTA

The Italian arms company Beretta has set up a factory in the US in order to service the military contract it won to supply the US Army with their 92F pistols.

■ COLT 1911 PISTOL DERIVATIVES

The popularity of the Colt 1911 design can be gauged by the number of US manufacturers making copies of it for commercial sale. Springfield Armoury, Auto Ordnance, Federal Ordnance, Caspian Arms, AMT, and Detonics all produce pistols in ·45 ACP and other calibres.

■ *The big LAR Grizzly ·45 Win Mag is an oversized Colt 1911 type pistol, beefed up for the powerful Magnum cartridge.*

LAR Manufacturing's "Grizzly" is an oversized 1911 which fires the ·45 Win Mag pistol cartridge; a similar stretching of the 1911 frame is used by Coonan Arms to produce its stainless steel ·357 Magnum Automatic pistol which fires the ·357 Magnum revolver cartridge. The Coonan was the result of a wager that a Colt-style pistol could not be made to reliably fire the ·357 Magnum round because of its length, pressure and rimmed case. Coonan has proved the doubters wrong with their powerful, accurate and strong package, albeit with a magazine capacity of only seven rounds.

■ BROWNING

The Browning Arms Company in Utah, US, is now part of the multinational Browning organization which has been closely involved with Fabrique Nationale d'Armes de Guerre (FN) in Belgium. In addition to distributing the Belgian- and Italian-made Browning pistols, they also manufacture the Buck Mark 22, Silhouette and Varmint ·22 pistols.

■ SINGLE SHOT PISTOLS

Single shot rimfire and centrefire pistols are made by an

assortment of American companies: Chipmunk Manufacturing, Competition Arms, Ithaca, MOA Corp, Remington, Rock Pistol Manufacturing (Merril), Thompson-Center, and Wichita Arms. European single shot pistols are virtually all ·22 RF for target use, and principally for free pistol, the Olympic discipline where 60 shots are fired in two and a half hours. American single shot pistols are usually made on a strong action which will accept interchangeable barrels in a range of centrefire rifle and handgun calibres. They are used for handgun hunting or silhouette shooting, where heavy steel plates cut in the shapes of birds and animals are shot at from 50–250 yards (45–230m). High energy cartridges are needed for silhouette shooting since the objective is to knock down the steel plates in order to score points.

The aftermarket grips and accessory manufacturer Pachmayr produces the Dominator kit which fits onto a standard Colt 1911 frame and converts it into a long-barrelled single shot pistol in five rifle and one revolver calibre.

■ US POCKET PISTOLS

The United States is unique in its number of manufacturers of small calibre pocket pistols made purely for close proximity personal defence. These range from the two-barrelled derringers, produced by the American Derringer Corporation in Texas and by Davis Industries, to small self-loading pistols in ·380 Auto such as the AMT Backup and the Grendel P-10. A number are made in ·25 Auto, of which the AMAC TP25 and the Raven MP-25 are examples. The small calibres used for most of these pocket pistols (apart from a few big bore derringers) are ineffective as manstoppers, but even so many sales are made to citizens who feel more comfortable if they have a gun of some sort around.

■ ASSAULT PISTOLS

There are also a number of manufacturers of assault pistols in the US. These are quite different from the conventional self-loading pistol in that they are usually modelled on or derived from straight-blowback open bolt machine pistols like the MAC10, with magazine capacities of up to 30 rounds. In order to separate them from fully automatic machine pistols and prevent conversion to fully automatic fire, assault pistols usually fire from a closed bolt and need the trigger to be released between each shot. The assault pistols made by Bushmaster, Encom, Federal Engineering, Holmes and Intratec all have vertical magazines which clip in below the breech. A recent newcomer from California, Instrument Co. who are known as the Calico, has a helical top mounted magazine on the M100P and M900P pistols. Available in ·22 LR and 9mm Luger, the Calico's radical design gives a far higher magazine capacity of 100 rounds in a small space.

■ *Opposite* Browning in the US produces their own Buck Mark ·22 pistols in addition to distributing the Belgian and Italian made Brownings.

■ *Top* The Calico M900 is a refreshing approach by an American manufacturer to the design of a new type of pistol.

SOUTH AMERICAN HANDGUNS

There are very few commercial handgun manufacturers in South America, and the two principal exporters, Taurus and Rossi, are both based in Brazil. At its factory in Porto Alegre, Forjas Taurus (The Bull Forge) produces a range of revolvers in calibres up to ·357 Magnum. The model choice totals 80 when variations of finish, frame size, sights and barrel are tallied. Taurus revolvers are similar in appearance to Smith & Wesson's "J" and "K" frame revolvers, but with a number of differences in the lockwork. Taurus also produces two versions of a copy of the Beretta 92F 9mm Luger self-loading pistol known as the PT-92 and PT-99, and a smaller Beretta-type ·380. One of South America's largest

■ The Brazilian factory of Armdeao Rossi produces a wide range of small and medium framed revolvers.

arms manufacturers, Amadeao Rossi, produces a range of 31 low priced revolvers in ·22 LR, ·32 S&W and ·38 Spl, which are also similar to Smith & Wesson's "J" and "K" framed models. A recent addition to Rossi's range is a ·357 Magnum revolver.

Fabrica Militar de Armes Portadiles has in the past produced Argentina's own service pistols at Santa Fé, based on the Colt 1911A1 (the Sistema Colt 1927 ·45 ACP) and the Browning GP35 (Pistola Browning PD), along with Hispano

■ One of West Germany's famous names, Walther still manufacture the pre-war designed PPK.

Argentino Fabrica de Autoviles SA, who made the Ballister Molina ·45 ACP Colt copy. All that is left today in Argentina is the Bersa factory, which makes a ·22 pistol (the 224) and a ·380 (9mmK), the Model 383.

WEST GERMANY

After the United States, the greatest proliferation of handgun manufacturers is found in West Germany, whose prowess in engineering and metallurgy is respected worldwide. A few of the old pre-war companies have started production again, and there have also been some fresh ideas in handgun design originating from new manufacturing plants.

■ WALTHER

In mainland Europe, the main thrust of handgun development since the turn of century has been in improving the self-loading pistol. Carl Walther of Ulm, West Germany, won world renown when it developed the first double action pistol, the PP Model, in 1929. The PP could be safely carried with the hammer down on a loaded chamber, but be fired instantly with a trigger cocked first shot, like a revolver. On firing the pistol cycled the action chambering a fresh round, leaving the hammer cocked for a subsequent single

■ *Willi Korth produces service and target revolves as well as works of art.*

action shots. The PP is still made today, as well as seven other sport and service pistol models in calibres ·22 LR, ·32 Auto (7·65mm), ·380 Auto (9mmK) and 9mm Luger. It is also made under licence in the United States, and like Smith & Wesson and Colt handguns is copied in many other countries. Walther also produces a small range of high quality target pistols in ·22 LR, ·22 Sh and ·32 S&W Long, which all use the same frame so that calibre conversion kits can be easily fitted and interchanged. Walther's FP model is a single shot Martini action ·22 LR pistol with an electronic trigger for the international Free Pistol target shooting discipline.

■ **HECKLER & KOCH**

One of the most innovative of the new post-war West German small arms manufacturers, Heckler & Koch, has applied the roller-locked breech from their successful self-loading rifles and machine pistols to a compact self-loading handgun, the P9S pistol, principally manufactured in 9mm Luger calibre. Not content with P9S, H&K also produces three versions of the PSP pistol originally designed for the West German Federal Police authority. Now known as the P7, the PSP is available in two full-power 9mm Luger versions with 8 round and 13 round magazine capacities, and as a training pistol which fires a lightweight plastic training bullet. The P7s have a unique and extremely safe firing mechanism which relies on the firer's grip to cock the action. If the pistol is dropped or the grip released for any reason, the pistol automatically decocks, eliminating the need for safety catches or double action trigger mechanisms. The P7 also uses gas pressure from the fired cartridge to delay the opening of the breech, a system known as gas-retarded blowback. The H&K VP 70 is an unusual high capacity straight blowback pistol in 9mm Luger which can be fired in three shot bursts when a special shoulder stock is fitted.

■ **SIG-SAUER**

J. P. Sauer and Sohn of Eckenforde produces the Sig-Sauer range of self-loading pistols, designed by the Swiss Industrial Company, SIG, but manufactured in Germany to facilitate easier export abroad. The Sig-Sauer P-220/225/226 "family" of large frame, delayed blowback self-loading pistols is made in three calibres, 9mm Luger, ·38 Super and ·45 ACP. The small light P-230 is only made in ·380 Auto (9mmK).

■ **MAUSER-WERKE**

The name Mauser is synonymous with the famous Model 1896 "Broomhandle" pistol and with seminal rifle actions. Today the name is perpetuated on a "Luger" Parabellum '08 replica, for which Mauser owns the manufacturing rights.

■ **OTHER WEST GERMAN PISTOL MANUFACTURERS**

The precision target rifle makers, Anschutz, produces a bolt

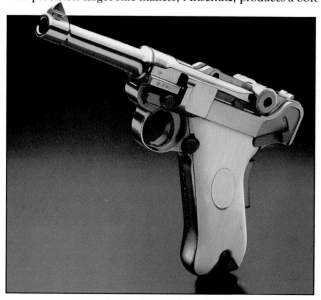

■ *The only handgun Mauser now produce is the Parabellum-Pistole 08 which is almost identical to George Luger's original P'08.*

action smallbore pistol known as the Exemplar, which has a five shot magazine capacity in ·22 LR and a four shot capacity in ·22 WMR.

Barrel-makers Peters Stahl have collaborated with Springfield Armoury in the United States to produce the Omega Pistol; it has a Springfield-manufactured 1911-type frame and trigger assembly, with the Peters Stahl "Multicaliber" slide which accepts a range of different calibre barrels.

Sub-calibre barrel insert manufacturer Erma-Werke produces ·22 LR versions of a Parabellum '08 type pistol known as the KPG22 and a ·380 Auto (9mmK) pistol called the KPG38.

Korriphila makes an extremely expensive, limited production, double action pistol, the HSP 701, which uses a delayed roller-lock action and is available in 9mm Luger, ·38 Spl-WC, ·38 Super and ·45 ACP.

■ GERMAN REVOLVERS

Despite the German emphasis on self-loading pistols, revolvers are still made in West Germany by Weirauch, who produce the Arminius models in calibres from ·22 LR to ·38 Spl, and by Willi Korth, a subsidiary of the Dynamit-Nobel conglomerate. Superbly engineered, the Korth revolvers are extremely accurate target weapons which are available in a range of calibres.

Hege-Waffenschmiede has recently begun producing another finely engineered revolver, the Army Match (International) ·44 black powder pistol. Like the Korth, this replica of the Remington 1858 percussion revolver is a very accurate match target revolver.

AUSTRIAN MANUFACTURERS

The revolutionary Glock 9mm Luger pistols are made in Vienna, Austria. Designed by an engineer with no previous experience of firearms, the Glock pistols make extensive use of plastics in the frame and magazine, and incorporate a number of new ideas in the firing mechanism. The result has been a simple and reliable high capacity handgun of very few parts, which was adopted as the Austrian service sidearm in 1983.

The Austrian engineering combine Steyr-Daimler-Puch AG also make a high capacity 9mm Luger pistol, the Steyr GB, which uses a fixed barrel and a gas-actuated, delayed blowback lock-up and cycling system.

SWITZERLAND

Swiss-made handguns are dominated by the products of the Small Arms Division of Schweizerische Industrie-Gesellschaft (SIG), the Swiss industrial company which also has an interest in Hämmerli. As well as designing the Sig-Sauer

pistols produced by Sauer in West Germany, SIG also manufactures the P210 9mm Luger service pistol, widely regarded as the finest self-loading pistol ever made. The Hämmerli range comprises precision "standard", "rapid fire" and "free" target pistols used by many international shooters. Hämmerli's new model 280 Standard Pistol has a substantial carbon fibre content which could lead the way for handgun designs of the future.

ITM of Solothurn produces a high quality copy of the CZ 75 pistol known as the AT 84 which has been re-engineered to take the new ·41 Action Express cartridge as well as the traditional 9mm Luger round.

■ *Switzerland's ITM produce a copy of the Czech CZ75 known as the AT 84 S which is in some respects better than the original.*

A recent newcomer to Swiss gunmaking is Morini, maker of a single shot free pistol, the CM-80, and a range of blowback standard rapid fire and centrefire target pistols with the unusual feature of a tubular magazine under the barrel, like a self-loading shotgun.

ITALIAN HANDGUNS

Italy claims that it invented the pistol in the 16th century, and whether or not that is correct, they certainly have a history of producing a large number of sporting and service smallarms, with the bulk of the manufacturers clustered around Gardone Val Trompia in Brescia, Northern Italy.

■ BERETTA

One of the oldest firearms manufacturers in the world is the company of Fabbrica d'Armi Pietro Beretta SpA, which can trace its origins back 400 years and is still owned by the same family who consolidated and expanded the business in the 19th century. Beretta's first pistol was the Model 1915, made during the First World War. Today, Beretta's Model

■ *Italy's largest handgun manufacturer, Beretta, has factories in the US and has manufactured in Brazil.*

92F in 9mm Luger is set to become one of the Western world's principal service sidearms, adopted by the American Army to replace the venerable 1911 Colt ·45 pistol in 1985, and in 1987 by the French Gendarmerie Nationale to replace the home-grown MAC50. The first Model 92 Beretta was announced in 1977, with a high magazine capacity – 15 rounds – and double action lockwork. Since then, Beretta has improved and refined it to suit the service specifications laid down by various countries, and the 92F is the current result. Despite convincingly winning the American military trials twice so far, the adoption of the Beretta has been tainted with accusations of political expediency, the contract allegedly being awarded in order to maintain American nuclear bases on mainland Italy. The United States are now about to embark on a further set of trials, for which the new Ruger P85 is being groomed as the Beretta's heir.

The success of the 92F has overshadowed the rest of the Beretta pistol range which includes the tiny 950 BS in ·22

Sh and ·25 Auto, the 84 and 85 DA's in ·380 Auto (9mmK), and the 93R, a 20 round capacity 9mm Luger pistol capable of firing three shot bursts.

Beretta produce an enclosed slide version of their model 84 for Browning, which is sold as the Browning BDA.

■ BERNADELLI

Also based in Gardone Val Trompia is the factory of Vincenzo Bernadelli SpA, established in 1865 and which can trace its line back to at least 1721. In 1984 Bernadelli launched the PO18 self-loading pistol, a well-made high capacity handgun in 9mm Luger and ·32 Auto (7·65mm) with which they hoped to establish themselves in a number of markets. Bernadelli produces the limited capacity Model 60 pistol in ·22 LR, ·32 Auto (7·65mm) and ·380 Auto (9mmK), and the Model 69 target pistol ·22 LR.

■ UBERTI

The main Italian contribution to revolver production is from Uberti, whose major product lines are replicas of early Colt percussion revolvers and Colt's cartridge Peacemaker model. Their sole "modern" revolver is similar to the discontinued Colt Diamondback in ·32 S&W Long and ·38 Spl.

■ OTHER ITALIAN MANUFACTURERS

The domination of Italian gunmaking by Beretta has not been to the exclusion of other smaller companies. Tanfoglio is one of these, whose TA90 9mm Luger pistol is a copy of the Czechoslovakian CZ75. Others, such as Targa, make smaller calibre self-loaders, while Renato Gamba SpA of Gardone VT produces the Trident Match 900 revolver and a licensed copy of the Mauser HSc in ·32 Auto and 9mm Luger, as well as its own versions of the CZ75.

■ *The smaller Italian gunmaker Bernadelli also produces high quality handguns.*

Benelli Armi SpA of Urbino introduced its military style B-76 9mm self-loader in 1977.

Armi San Marco is the "other" principle producer of Italian replica black powder revolvers, concentrating on Colt and Remington models. The Italian ammunition manufacturer Fiocchi is marketing the Pardini-Fiocchi, a ·22 LR self-loading target pistol which is gaining a strong following at club and international level for precision shooting in Europe.

More high grade target pistols in ·22 LR, ·22 Short, and ·32 S&W Long-WC are made in Italy by FAS. Armi San Paolo in Concesio produces a range of double action revolvers which were previously made by Sauer & Sohn in West Germany.

SPANISH HANDGUNS

Like Italy, Spain has a long tradition of gunmaking, although much of it is centred on shotguns rather than hand-guns. The companies that do make handguns have concentrated in the past on copying other European and American models and have not had a particularly good reputation. Recently, however, some good, new designs have been emanating from the factories.

■ *The modern Spanish Star pistols are well made, reliable and competitively priced.*

■ GABILONDO Y CIA (LLAMA)

Based in Vitoria, Gabilondo manufactures the Commanche III and Commanche V revolvers under the Llama name, similar in appearance to Smith & Wesson's medium and large frame models. The Commanche V is available in ·357 and ·44 Magnum, with the smaller Commanche III made in ·357 only. Other copies of well-proven American hand-guns are the Llama IX-A and XI-B, which have more than

■ *The Browning Hi Power is still made in Belgium by FN. Illustrated is the Mk2 with an ambidextrous safety catch.*

a passing resemblance to Colt's 1911 single action pistols, and the small frame auto pistols which are scaled-down versions of the same. The Llama Omni is a recently introduced double action self-loading pistol in 9mm Luger and ·45 ACP. While the Omni owes a lot to Browning's basic locked-breech design, it has some new features, including a ball-jointed firing pin and two sear bars, one for single action firing and one for double action.

■ UNCETA Y CIA (ASTRA)

At its factory in Guernica, Unceta also makes copies of Smith & Wesson's medium and large frame revolvers under its own Astra trade name. Established as gunmakers in 1908, Astra produced a selective-fire copy of the Mauser 1896 in the 1930s which effectively forced the Mauser company to make one as well. Astra has in the past supplied the Spanish military with many of their weapons but they are now losing that ground to Star. Its A-90 double action pistol is made in 9mm Luger and ·45 ACP, the A-60 in ·380 Auto (9mmK), and the Constable in ·22 LR and ·380 Auto (9mmK).

■ STAR-BONIFACIO (STAR)

Star produce high quality, compact, military and personal defence pistols in 9mm Luger and ·45 ACP, as well as a simple, reliable, self-loading ·22 target pistol, the FR. The double action service pistols 30M and 30PK have a magazine capacity of 15 rounds of 9mm Luger, the BM and BKM hold nine rounds of 9mm Luger, and the lightweight PD will take six rounds of ·45 ACP.

■ OLIMPIC

The Olimpic rapid fire pistol is a ported-barrel target pistol chambered for ·22 Short, made in Spain.

■ *The new British Victory pistol features easily changed calibres on the same frame, with a range of barrel lengths.*

FRANCE

France is a large military weapons exporter, and there are several small arms factories in France. The number producing handguns has been rationalized over recent years, and the adoption of the Beretta 92F by the Gendarmerie Nationale (to be made under licence by the national arsenal Manufacture D'Armes de Saint-Etienne) will probably cause further curtailment.

At Manufacture d'Armes de Pyrenees of Hendaye, the trade name Unique is used for its popular target pistols, of which the DES-69 ·22 is the most widely known.

The present French service pistol is the Model PA-15 Auto Pistol in 9mm Luger made at Manufacture d'Armes Automatiques in Bayonne.

The high-precision Manurhin, solid frame double action revolvers, are made by Manufacture de Machines du Haut-Rhin, Mulhouse, and are available in ·32 S&W Long, ·38 Spl and ·357 Magnum.

BELGIUM

The Fabrique Nationale d'Armes de Guerre (FN) factory at Herstal, Belgium, began its relationship with Browning's designed pistols when the Model 1900 was produced at the turn of the century. Browning's name has become synonymous with FN pistols, and the most famous Browning pistol of them all, the 9mm High Power or GP35, was developed from Browning's drawings after his death in 1926. The single action, high-capacity High Power became one of the most popular service pistols in the world, and is still used by many countries' armed forces, including those of Great Britain. Browning's delayed blowback lock up has been copied in various forms by many other handgun manufacturers as it is both simple and reliable.

FN has been working on a double action version of the High Power for many years in order to compete in the new round of military trials, and it has finally produced an all-new pistol, the FN35DA, the parts of which will not interchange with the old GP35. A few models of the 35DA have been sold in the United States, but the pistol is not yet widely available.

The intertwined company structures of Browning and FN have been recently overhauled and they are now two separate businesses. Browning's head office is still in Belgium, and it markets commercially through its subsidiaries. FN make the High Power in its various guises – the Vigilante, Sport (with adjustable sights), Competition (long barrel and barrel weight), and Mark Two (with ambidextrous safety). Other Belgian-made Browning pistols are the ·22 LR target models, the International and the Practice 150.

Browning also sells the BDA, a high-capacity straight blowback ·380 Auto (9mmK) pistol based on Beretta's model 81 & 84 design, with a solid slide and made for Browning by Beretta.

FN no longer sells pistols direct to the civilian market – now handled by Browning – but they still supply GP35 handguns under military contract.

GREAT BRITAIN

Great Britain has four manufacturers of handguns, all based in England. Weslake Engineering has taken over production of the Britarms target pistols and has given them a new lease of life. Modern & Antique Firearms in Bournemouth produces the Kengil single shot, long-range pistols, and May of London still makes Jurek ·22 single shot, target pistols to order. The most exciting new British development has been the establishment of a new company, Victory Arms, at Northampton who have designed and manufactured the Victory MC5 system. The MC5 has been designed as a fully ambidextrous, multi-calibre, double action service and sporting self-loading handgun which can be stripped without tools in seconds. Calibre changes require only a replacement barrel and magazine, and there is no need to replace the slide. Barrels are available in three lengths, 4⅜ ins (111mm), 5⅞ ins (149mm) and 7½ ins (191mm). The calibre options are 9mm Luger, ·38 Super, ·41 Action Express and ·45 ACP. Magazine capacity with 9mm and ·38 Super is 17 rounds, 12 rounds in ·41AE and 10 rounds in ·45 ACP.

In 1988 it was announced that two more handguns were to be manufactured in Great Britain. The first is a licensed version of the ITM AT84 pistol, itself a copy of the Czech CZ 75. The second is the PMX90 Varan, a single action self-loading pistol originally intended for production in South Africa. The designer, Tony Blackshaw, returned to Great Britain in 1988 with the intention of co-manufacturing the pistol with a British gunshop proprietor.

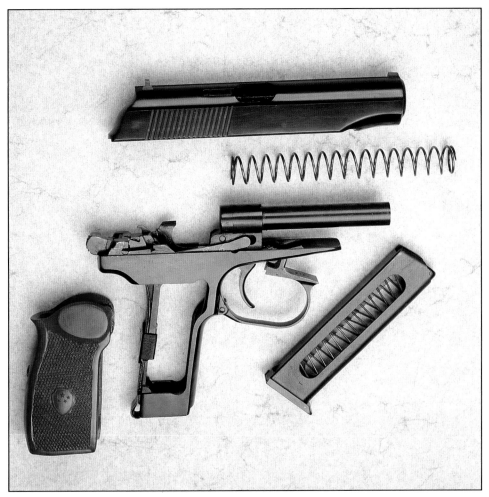

■ *The Eastern Bloc produces a small range of handguns. The Makarov pistol is a 9mm service pistol cloned from the Walther PP after World War II.*

■ *The British small arms manufacturer, Sterling, designed and prototyped a ·357 Magnum revolver which did not go into production. The revolver illustrated is unique, a prototype with a 6 in barrel and target sights.*

OTHER EUROPEAN MANUFACTURERS

Scattered throughout Europe are a number of handgun manufacturers who principally supply the military; for example, both Husquvarna Vapenfabrik in Sweden and VKT in Finland have made versions of the Lahti 9mm Luger service pistol. Others are sporting pistol producers, such as SAKO, also of Finland, who make the Triace three calibre target pistol, and Saxhøj of Denmark who make the Agner 80 ·22 LR target pistol.

The Krikkale pistol is a Turkish version of the Walther PP, made in ·32 Auto (7·65mm) and ·380 (9mmK) by Makina ve Kimeya Endustrisi Kurumu, Ankara.

ISRAEL

Israel has rapidly developed an arms and ammunition manufacturing capability in order to supply its own forces in the Middle East. In order to keep the machinery working during "quiet" periods, Israel Military Industries at Ramat Hasheron has developed a large gas-operated self-loading pistol to be marketed in Europe and America. The Desert Eagle pistol will fire either the ·357 Magnum or ·44 Magnum revolver cartridge, calibres that IMI makes for

export. The Desert Eagle is a heavy, bulky handgun for which the principal application is handgun hunting or metallic silhouette shooting, especially with the optional long barrel and telescopic sights. IMI also makes a closed bolt blowback assault pistol, the UZI Pistol in 9mm Luger and ·45 ACP. The UZI Pistol is derived from the highly successful open bolt UZI machine pistol.

Sardius Industries in Ramat-Gan has made a 9mm blowback pistol which employs extensive use of sheet metal stampings to reduce the price.

EASTERN BLOC

Very few of the handguns made in the Eastern Bloc are exported commercially to the West, and most of the service pistol samples which turn up are trophies of war. Russian-made Margolin (Vostock) ·22 LR target pistols are available in the West, but the service issue Makarov 9mmM and PSM 5·45mm pistols, and TOZ free pistols and revolvers are not. Yugoslavia produces a locally-made version of the Tokarev pistol, and Poland manufactures the PM63 9mmM pistol, a cross between the Soviet Makarov and a Walther PP.

BRNO in Czechoslovakia has taken a different approach to that of the Soviet Union, and developed the Browning- and SIG-based CZ 75 and CZ 85 double action 9mm Luger pistols for export; in doing so, it has produced one of the best 9mm handguns available today. Because of import restrictions on Eastern Bloc products in some Western countries, the CZ 75 has been copied in Italy and Switzerland in order to capitalize on its popularity. BRNO produces a compact, 15 round capacity, straight blowback pistol, the CZ 83, in ·32 Auto (7·65mm) and in ·380 Auto (9mmK), as well as distributing the Czech-made Drulov and Pav ·22 target pistols.

The Czechoslovakian Skorpion selective fire pistol, issued to their army, is not available (officially) in the West.

FEG in Budapest, Hungary, manufactures and exports two 9mm Luger pistols based on the Browning High Power, the P9R double action and the FP9 single action, in addition to a small auto pistol, the PPH in ·32 and ·380 Auto.

CHINA

Having emerged from the cultural revolution, China is starting to trade with the rest of the world again. The state-owned arms factory Norinco is one of the largest arms manufacturers in the world and included in its range are nine handguns, four service pistols and five sporting handguns. The designs are heavily influenced by the USSR and the service pistols are cloned from the Tokarev, Makarov and Russian "Walther" based pistols. Three of the sport pistols are self-loading ·22s based on the Margolins, with one single shot Free Pistol in ·22. Norinco's ·22s have proved very successful in international competition in recent years, winning Olympic medals and setting world record scores. The sole revolver is a target handgun chambered in 7·62mm.

■ *The latest Grizzly pistols will chamber a high velocity ·357 Wildcat round.*

PHILIPPINES

Armscor of the Philippines produces a basic 4 ins double action revolver in ·38 Spl.

JAPAN

New Nambu Models 57A (9mm Luger Colt type pistol), 57B (·32 Auto Browning 1922 type pistol), and 60 (five shot ·38 Spl DA revolver) are made for police and military use by Shin Chuo Kogyo in Tokyo and are not available to civilians.

■ *Brazil's Taurus revolver looks similar to Smith & Wesson's but there are internal differences in the lockwork.*

SINGLE SHOT & BOLT ACTION PISTOLS

The single barrelled pistols of the 16th century were the forbears of the modern handgun and many of their qualities of simplicity, reliability and strength are replicated in the single shot cartridge pistols that are being produced today.

Modern, single shot pistols are not used for defence or for military assaults but for sporting purposes: either target shooting or handgun hunting. In Europe, target shooting broadly follows the doctrines of the Union International de Tir, the UIT, which encompasses international rimfire and centrefire target pistol shooting. All of the centrefire disciplines, and all but one of the rimfire ones, require the delivery of multiple shots in a short time, so the single shot pistol is not suitable, due to its slow speed of use.

The Olympic discipline, Free Pistol, has no such constraints, since 60 shots need to be fired at 50 metres in two and a half hours. This has led to the development of highly specialized, single shot pistols with "orthopaedic" grips to wrap around the hand, and electronic release triggers for the shortest possible lock time – the time taken for the cartridge to be ignited from when the trigger is squeezed. All free pistols are in ·22 LR rimfire calibre. Most European single shot pistols are chambered for ·22 LR; exceptions to this are the bolt action Anschutz Exemplar, which is also available in ·22 WMR, and the hand-built British Kengils,

■ *Customized SSK conversion of single shot Thompson/Center Contender.*

used for long range pistol shooting and made in calibres up to ·308 Win.

In the United States, however, there has been far more scope for large calibre, single shot pistols since the introduction of long range target shooting at heavy steel plate targets (known as silhouette shooting), and the acceptance of handgun hunting for large and small game. The strength of single shot pistols is very high in relation to their weight, so very powerful cartridges can be chambered, including a number of rifle calibres.

■ *American single shot pistols like the RPM XL are used at long range for hunting or for steel target shooting.*

■ *Ultra Light Arms Reb Hunters bolt action pistol.*

There are many diverse action types available for single shot pistols despite the apparent simplicity of the single chambered barrel. One of the most popular actions is the "break top", which hinges upwards just forward of the breech when unlatched, giving access to the chamber. This allows a simple hammer and trigger to be used in a common frame, and a range of barrels can be easily interchanged. This versatility is best illustrated by the Thompson/Center Contender pistol which can use the same action for calibres from ·22 LR up to ·357 Herret and ·44 Magnum. The Contender action is used by hunting pistol builder J. D. Jones of SSK Industries who has developed the SSK Handcannons which fire a range of "wildcat", non-standard calibres for hunting.

Bolt actions derived from rifles are used on some single shot pistols such as the Remington XP-100 for strength

■ *Top* Uberti Rolling Block pistol.

■ *Below* MOA Falling Block pistol.

ALPHABETICAL LISTING OF CURRENTLY-PRODUCED SINGLE SHOT PISTOLS AND BOLT ACTION CARTRIDGE FIRING PISTOLS

Model	Type of action	Calibre(s)	Capacity	Barrel length(s)	Sights
ANSCHUTZ WEST GERMANY					
Exemplar	Bolt Action	·22 LR, ·22 WMR	5 (·22 LR), 4 (·22 WMR)	10" (254mm)	Adjustable
CHIPMUNK US					
Silhouette	Bolt Action	·22 LR	One	14⅞" (375mm)	Adjustable
COMPETITION ARMS US					
Competitor	Break Top	·22 LR, ·223/5·56mm 7mm TCU, 7mm Int, ·357 Max, ·41 Mag, ·44 Mag, ·454 Casull, ·375 Super Mag + Special Orders	One	10·5" (267mm), 14" (356mm)	Adjustable
DRULOV CZECHOSLOVAKIA					
70 & 75	Rotating bolt	·22 Sh, ·22 Lo, ·22LR	One	9" (229mm)	Adjustable
GAMBA ITALY					
Air Match	Falling block	·22 LR	One	10·4" (265mm)	Adjustable
HÄMMERLI SWITZERLAND					
150	Martini	·22 LR	One	11¼"	Adjustable
152 electronic	Martini, electronic trigger	·22 LR	One	11¼"	Adjustable
ITHACA US					
20 & 30 X-Caliber	Break top	·22 LR, ·223/5·56mm, ·35 Rem, ·357 Mag, ·357 Max, ·44 Mag	One	10", 15"	Adjustable
MAY'S ENGLAND					
Jurek	Sliding breech	·22 LR	One	To order	Adjustable
MOA US					
Maximum	Falling Block	·22 Hornet to ·44 Mag (20 options)	One	10½", 14"	Adjustable
MODERN & ANTIQUE FIREARMS ENGLAND					
Kengil	Slide action	Any to order up to ·308 Win	One	12" std, others to order	None (used with telescopic sights)
MORINI SWITZERLAND					
CM-80	Martini	·22 LR	One	11"	Adjustable
NORINCO CHINA					
MS-01 Free pistol	Martini	·22 LR	One	11·4"	Adjustable
REMINGTON US					
XP-100 Silhouette	Bolt Action	7mm BR, ·35 Rem	One	14¾"	None (drilled and tapped for telescopic sight mount)
XP-100 "Varmint Special"	Bolt Action	·223 (5·56mm)	One	10½"	None (drilled and tapped for telescopic sight mount)
XP-100 Custom	Bolt Action	·223 (5·56mm), 7mm-08, ·35 Rem	One	14½"	Adjustable Bomar
RPM US					
XL	Break top	·22 LR to ·45–70 (22 option)	One	8", 10", 10¾", 12", 14"	Adjustable
TEXAS US					
Jezebel	Break top	·22 Sh, ·22 Lo, ·22LR	One	6"	Fixed
TOZ USSR					
35		·22 LR	One	10·5"	Adjustable
THOMPSON/CENTER US					
Contender	Break top	·22 Sh to ·45 Colt/·410 (22 options)	One	10", 14"	Adjustable
UBERTI ITALY					
Rolling Block	Rolling Block	·22 LR, ·22 WMR, ·22 Hornet, ·357 Mag	One	9⅞"	Adjustable
ULTRA LIGHT US					
20 Reb Hunter	Bolt Action	·22–250 to ·308 Win	Five	14"	None, telescopic sight mount included

ALPHABETICAL LISTING OF CURRENTLY-PRODUCED SINGLE SHOT PISTOLS AND BOLT ACTION CARTRIDGE FIRING PISTOLS

Model	Type of action	Calibre(s)	Capacity	Barrel length(s)	Sights
WALTHER WEST GERMANY					
FP	Martini	·22 LR	One	11″	Adjustable
WICHITA US					
MK-40 Silhouette	Bolt Action	·22–250, 7mm IHMSA, ·308 Win	One	13″	Adjustable Multi Range
Silhouette	Bolt Action LH & RH	·22–250, 7mm IHMSA, ·308 Win	One	10¾″, 15″	Adjustable Multi Range
Classic	Bolt Action	Any up to ·308 Win	One	11¼″	Adjustable Micro
Hunter & International	Break Top	·22 LR, ·22 WMR, 7mmINT, ·30–30 Win, ·32 H&R Mag, ·357 Mag, ·357 Max	One	10½″	International – Adj, Hunter – 'Scope mount only

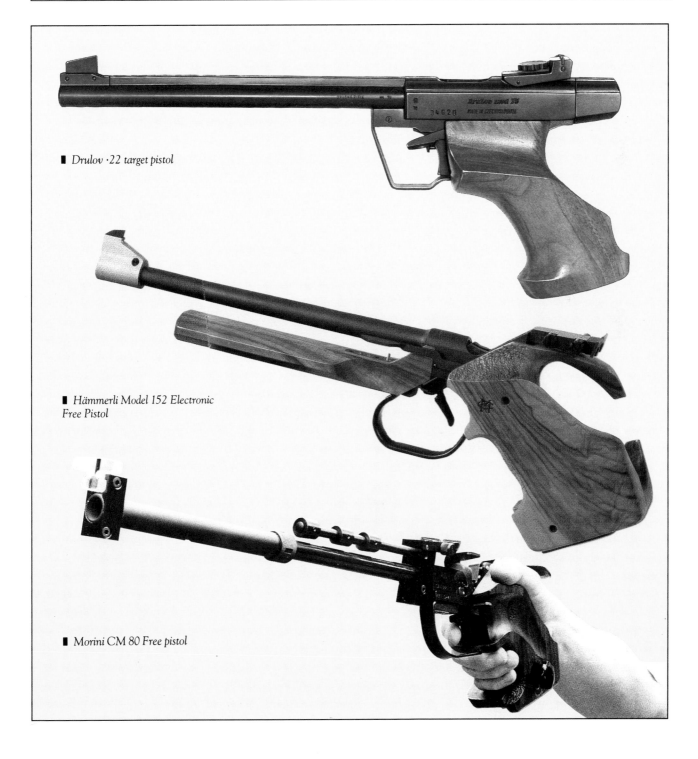

■ *Drulov ·22 target pistol*

■ *Hämmerli Model 152 Electronic Free Pistol*

■ *Morini CM 80 Free pistol*

■ **Top** *Walther FP Free Pistol*

■ **Below** *A Thompson Contender in 6·5mm JDJ calibre brought down this Cape Hartebeste at 275 yards.*

with high powered rifle cartridges. Like the Contender, the XP-100 has been used as a base for a number of "wildcat" calibre handguns. One lesson that is slow to be learnt by some bolt action pistol makers is that for a right-handed shooter, it is far easier to operate the bolt with the left hand while maintaining a strong grip on the pistol with the gun hand. Many of the rifle-derived actions still have "right-handed" bolts which are the norm for rifles. A few manufacturers produce limited magazine capacity bolt action handguns.

The falling block action was originally made for early 19th-century rifles, but, like the bolt action, has found favour with some single shot pistol manufacturers because of its strength. The MOA Corporation once made a test pistol chambered for ·460 Weatherby Magnum, the world's most powerful commercial rifle cartridge, in order to check the robustness of its falling block action. The pistol was fired in a machine rest (no one would volunteer to hand fire it!) and when the smoke and dust had cleared, the pistol was still intact, but it had ripped the machine rest out of its mountings. Gamba use a modified falling block in its Air Match free pistol.

DERRINGERS

The derringer is a purely defensive handgun. Its origination and name is attributed to the Philadelphian gunsmith Henry Deringer who made short-barrelled, large calibre single shot pistols in the 1820s. While a few replicas of the original single shot Deringer-style percussion and cartridge pistols are still made, the modern term "derringer" (with two "r"s) usually means a multi-barrelled or manually-operated magazine pistol which is small and easily concealed.

The most prolific manufacturer is the American Derringer Corporation, which makes seven two-barrelled, top hinge models in calibres from ·22 LR up to ·45–70 Govt and ·410 shotgun. They also make the Semmerling LM-4, a manually-operated repeater in 9mm Luger or ·45 ACP.

A four-barrelled break top ·22 LR and ·22 WMR derringer has been made by Advantage Arms, and this incorporated a rotating firing pin to fire the barrels in turn with each pull of the double action trigger.

Most derringers are made in the United States where there is a good market among those who gain comfort from the possession of a small, cheap, lightweight, small calibre pistol. While all derringers can injure or stop aggressors

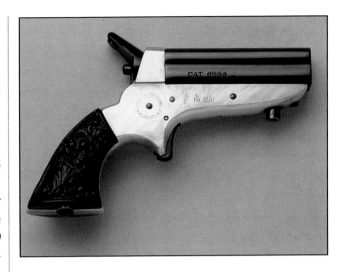

Above & below *Uberti Four Shot Sharps Derringer, ·22 LR*

with correct shot placement, this is beyond the skill of most of the people who carry them, and they would be wise to examine the concept of the original Deringer pistols: it relied on the immense stopping power of a large calibre bullet to carry out the design function.

DERRINGER MANUFACTURER LISTING

Model	Type of action	Calibre(s)	Capacity	Barrel length(s)	Sights
AMERICAN DERRINGER MODELS US					
Model 1	Swing up two shot	·22 LR, ·22 WMR, ·22 Hornet, ·223/5·56mm, ·30 Lu, ·30–30 Win, ·32 AutoP/7·65mm, ·38 Sup, ·380 Auto/9mmK, ·38 Spl, 9mmV/9×18, 9mmLu, 9mm Fed, ·357 Mag, ·357 Max, ·41 Mag, ·38–40, ·44–40 Win, ·44 Spl, ·44 Am, ·44 Mag, ·45 Colt, ·45 ACP, ·410 Gua-2½″	Two	3″	Blade front, no rear
Model 3	Swing up two shot	·38 Spl	Two	2½″	Blade front, no rear
Model 4	Swing up two shot	·410 Gua-3″ &/or ·45 Colt, ·410 Gua-3″ plus ·45 Colt or ·45–70	Two	4·1″	Blade front, no rear
Model 6	Swing up two shot	·410 Gua-3″, ·45 Colt	Two	6″	Blade front, no rear
Model 7	Aluminium swing up two shot	·22 LR, ·32 S&W Lo, ·32 H&R Mag, ·380 Auto/9mmK, ·38 S&W, ·38 Spl, ·44 Spl	Two	3″	Blade front, no rear
Model 10	Swing up two shot	·38 Spl, ·45 ACP, ·45 Colt	Two	3″	Blade front, no rear
Model 11	Swing up two shot	·38 Spl	Two	3″	Blade front, no rear
Texas Commemorative	Swing up two shot, brass frame, stainless barrel	·38 Spl, ·44–40, ·44 Am, ·45 Colt	Two	3″	Blade front, no rear
Semmerling LM-4	Manually operated repeater	9mm Lu, ·45 ACP	Seven (9mm Lu), Five (·45 ACP)	3⅝″	Fixed
DAVIS INDUSTRIES US					
Derringer	Swing up two shot	·22 LR, ·22 WMR, ·25 Auto/6·35mm, ·32 Auto/7·65mm	Two	2·4″	Fixed
EXCEL US					
DA Derringer	Trigger cocked, swing up	·38 Spl	Two	3″	Fixed
INTRATEC US					
Companion	Swing out two shot, trigger cocked, moulded plastic stock	·32 H&R Mag, ·38 Spl, ·357 Mag	Two	3″	Fixed
LJUTIC US					
LJ II	Side by side two shot, trigger cocked, stainless steel	·22 WMR	Two	2¾″	Fixed
TANARMI ITALY (assembled in US)					
O/U Derringer	Swing up two shot	·38 Spl	Two	3″	Fixed
UBERTI ITALY					
New Maverick	Swing up two shot	·38 Spl	Two	2¾″	Fixed
Sharps Derringer	Slide open, trigger cocked, rotating firing pin	·22 Short	Four	2½″	Fixed

REVOLVERS

The cartridge revolver is where the modern repeating handgun began, and double action revolvers are the most popular handguns in use today for personal defense and law enforcement. They make fine sporting weapons, along with the older design single action revolvers, for target and hunting use. The trigger-cocking method of indexing and firing is one operational option of the double action revolver, and this has been around since the days of the trigger-cocked percussion pepperboxes. The merging of the alternatives of trigger-cocking for rapid shooting or hammer-cocking (usually known as single action) for slower precise shots to create the true double action revolver was achieved in the middle of the 19th century; from then on, the revolver created an unrivalled reputation as a repeating handgun of reliability and accuracy with a wide range of ammunition.

Single action revolvers have a much simpler action but are slower to shoot accurately, due to the need to manually cock the hammer before firing. Modern handguns with hammer-cocked single actions work in an almost identical fashion to Colt's original designs early in the 19th century, with the addition of safety features such as hammer blocks and the use of modern materials for their manufacture. Replicas of 19th-century revolvers are used for sporting target shooting and for pure nostalgia, while modern versions with adjustable sights and stronger frames find favour with silhouette shooters, hunters, and for target shooting.

Today, the double action revolver can be found in all spheres of shooting, with the exception of military forces; they generally prefer self-loading pistols for their high magazine capacity and ammunition compatibility with other fully-automatic smallarms.

The most common design of double action revolvers is the Smith & Wesson pattern, produced in high volume in the United States and copied throughout the world.

Transfer-Bar

Firing Pin

Hammer Pivot

Mainspring Strut

Cylinder Latch

Trigger and Cylinder Latch Pivot

Trigger

Trigger Spring

■ *Top left* *Ruger's Blackhawk is a modern single action revolver making use of hammer blocks and music wire springs.*

■ *Left* *Armi San Paolo "Sauer" Service model*

57

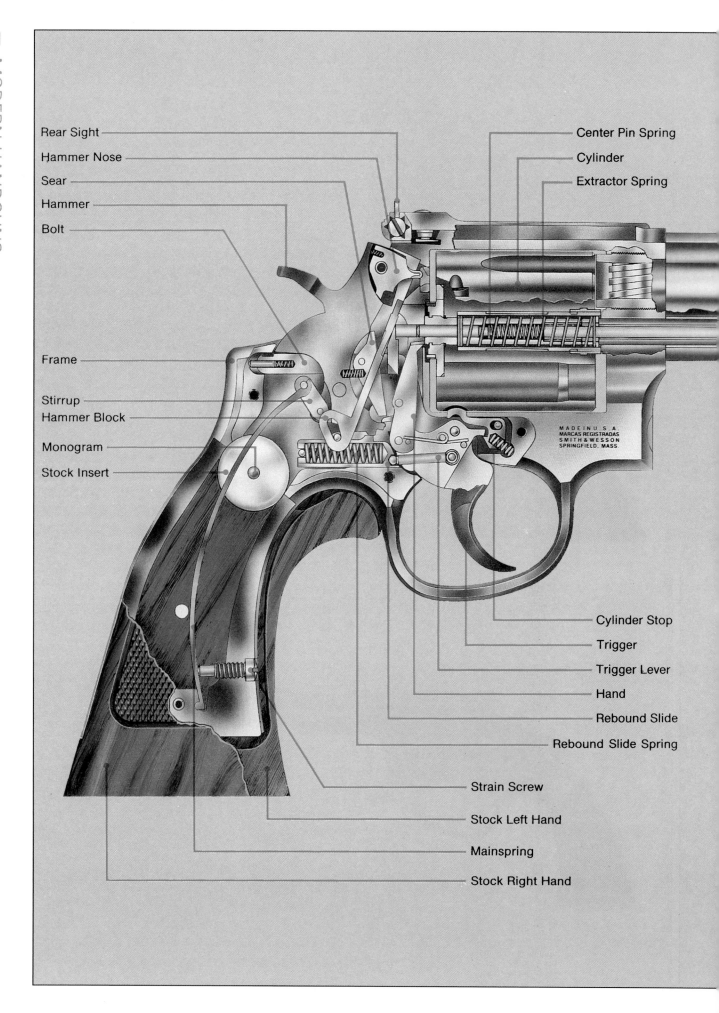

Rear Sight

Hammer Nose

Sear

Hammer

Bolt

Frame

Stirrup

Hammer Block

Monogram

Stock Insert

Center Pin Spring

Cylinder

Extractor Spring

MADE IN U.S.A.
MARCAS REGISTRADAS
SMITH & WESSON
SPRINGFIELD, MASS.

Cylinder Stop

Trigger

Trigger Lever

Hand

Rebound Slide

Rebound Slide Spring

Strain Screw

Stock Left Hand

Mainspring

Stock Right Hand

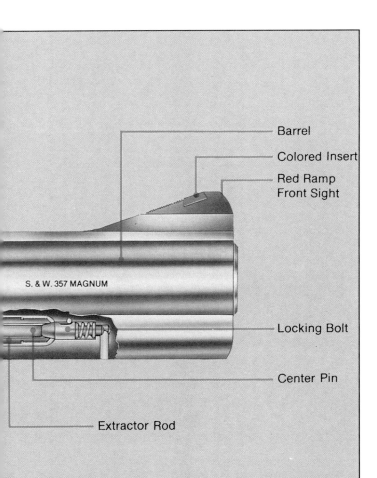

Barrel
Colored Insert
Red Ramp
Front Sight

S. & W. 357 MAGNUM

Locking Bolt

Center Pin

Extractor Rod

■ *Above* Charter Arms Bulldog
"Pug" .44 Special.

■ *Left* Smith & Wesson's double
action revolvers are the most
popular (and widely copied) in the
world.

DOUBLE ACTION REVOLVERS

Model	Calibre(s)	Capacity	Barrel length(s)	Sights	Finish
ARMSCOR PHILIPPINES					
Armscor	·38 Spl	Six	4"	Adj, windage	Blue
ARMI SAN PAOLO ITALY					
Compact	·32 S&W Long, ·38 Spl	Six	2"	Fixed	Blue
Service	·32 S&W Long, ·38 Spl	Six	2", 4"	Fixed	Blue
Service Special	·22 LR, ·32 S&W Long, ·38 Spl	Six	4", 6"	Adjustable	Blue
Competitor	·22 LR, ·32 S&W Long, ·38 Spl	Six	6", Vent rib	Adjustable	Blue
ASTRA SPAIN					
357 Magnum	·357 Mag	Six	3", 4", 6", 8½"	Adjustable	Blue
Models 44 & 45	·44 Mag & ·45 Colt	Six	6"	Adjustable	Blue
Terminator	·44 Mag	Six	2½"	Adjustable	Blue
CHARTER ARMS US					
Bulldog	·44 Spl	Five	2½", 3"	Fixed	Blue or Stainless
Bulldog Pug	·44 Spl	Five	2½"	Fixed	Blue or Stainless
Pathfinder	·22 LR	Six	3", 4", 6"	Adjustable	Blue (4" & 6"), Stainless (3")
Police Bulldog	·32 H&R Mag, ·38 Spl	Six	4", 4" Bull Barrel	Adjustable (·32) and fixed (·38)	Blue (all) or Stainless (·38 only)
Police Undercover	·32 H&R Mag, ·38 Spl	Six	2"	Fixed	Blue or Stainless
Off Duty	·38 Spl, ·22 LR	5 (·38), 6 (·22)	2"	Fixed	Blue or Stainless
Target Bulldog	·357 Mag, ·44 Spl	Five	4"	Adjustable	
Undercover	·32 S&W Long, ·38 Spl	Five (·32), Six (·38 Spl)	2" (·32), 2" & 3" (·38 Spl)	Five	Blue or Stainless (2" Brl. only)

DOUBLE ACTION REVOLVERS

Model	Calibre(s)	Capacity	Barrel Length(s)	Sights	Finish
COLT US					
King Cobra	·357 Mag	Six	2½", 4", 6"	Adjustable	Blue (4" & 6") or Stainless (all)
Python	·357 Mag	Six	2½", 4", 6", 8"	Adjustable	Blue (all) or Stainless (2½–6")
GAMBA ITALY					
Super 2½"	·32 S&W Long, ·38 Spl	Six	2½", 3"	Fixed	Blue
Super 4"	·32 S&W Long, ·38 Spl	Six	4" Vent rib	Adjustable	Blue
Trident Match 900	·32 S&W Long, ·38 Spl	Six	6"	Adjustable	Matte black
KORTH WEST GERMANY					
Combat	·22 LR, ·22 WMR, ·32 H&R Mag, ·357 Mag. Also available with interchangeable cylinders adding calibres ·32 S&W Long, 9mm Luger and 9×21mm	Six	3", 4", 5¼", 6"	Fixed	Blue, stainless
Target	·22 LR, ·32 S&W Long, ·38 Spl, ·357 Mag. Also available with interchangeable cylinders adding ·22 WMR, ·32 H&R Mag, 9mm Luger and 9×21mm	Six	4", 5¼", 6", 8"	Adjustable	Blue, stainless
LLAMA SPAIN					
Comanche III	·357 Mag	Six	4", 6"	Adjustable	Blue
Super Comanche V	·357 Mag, ·44 Mag	Six	4", 6", 8"	Adjustable	Blue
MANURHIN FRANCE					
MR 32	·32 S&W Long	Six	6"	Adjustable	Blue
MR 73	·357 Mag & 9mm Lu	Six	6"	Adjustable	Blue
NEW ENGLAND FIREARMS US					
H&R Revolvers	·22 LR, ·32 H&R Mag	Nine (·22), five (·32)	2½" & 4"	Fixed	Blue or nickel
NORINCO CHINA					
ZS-01	7·62mm Nagent	Six	6"	Adjustable	Blue

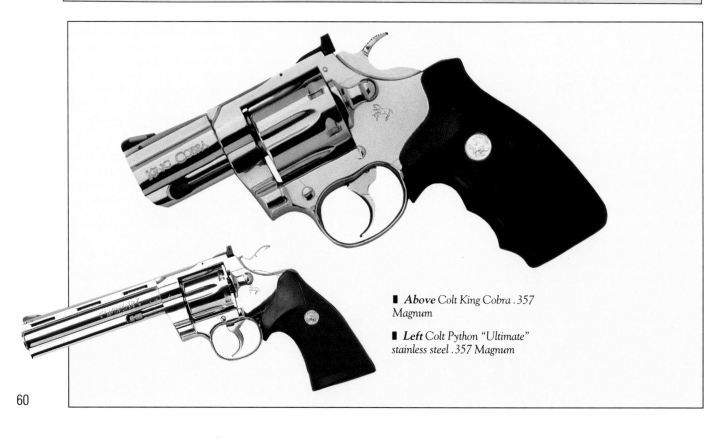

■ **Above** Colt King Cobra .357 Magnum

■ **Left** Colt Python "Ultimate" stainless steel .357 Magnum

▮ **Top** Gamba Trident 900 .38
Special

▮ **Middle** Gamba Trident Super
4-in .38 Spl

▮ **Bottom** New England H&R
revolver

■ *Top and middle* Ruger
GP100 ·357 Magnum.

■ *Bottom* Ruger Redhawk ·44 Magnum.

DOUBLE ACTION REVOLVERS

Model	Finish	Calibre(s)	Capacity	Barrel length	Sights
ROSSI Models BRAZIL					
27	Blue	·38 Spl	5	2″	Fixed
31	Blue	·38 Spl	5	4″	Fixed
33	Blue	·38 Spl	5	3″	Fixed
87	Stainless	·38 Spl	5	2″	Fixed
88	Stainless	·38 Spl	5	3″	Fixed
881	Stainless	·38 Spl	5	4″	Fixed
20	Blue	·32 S&W Lo	6	3″	Fixed
28	Blue	·32 S&W Lo	6	2″	Fixed
42	Blue	·22 LR	6	2″	Fixed
43	Blue	·22 LR	6	3″	Fixed
85	Stainless	·38 Spl	6	3″	Adjustable
89	Blue	·32 S&W Lo	6	3″	Fixed
94	Blue	·38 Spl	6	3″	Fixed
95	Blue	·38 Spl	6	3″	Adjustable
97	Blue	·357 Mag	6	3″	Adjustable
283	Stainless	·32 S&W Lo	6	6″	Adjustable
293	Blue	·32 S&W Lo	6	6″	Adjustable
483	Stainless	·22 LR	6	6″	Adjustable
493	Blue	·22 LR	6	6″	Adjustable
511	Stainless	·22 LR	6	6″	Adjustable
851	Stainless	·38 Spl	6	4″	Adjustable
853	Stainless	·38 Spl	6	6″	Adjustable
854	Stainless	·38 Spl	6	2″	Adjustable
941	Blue	·38 Spl	6	4″	Fixed
944	Blue	·38 Spl	6	2″	Fixed
951	Blue	·38 Spl	6	4″	Adjustable
953	Blue	·38 Spl	6	6″	Adjustable
954	Blue	·38 Spl	6	2″	Adjustable
971	Blue	·357 Mag	6	4″	Adjustable
974	Blue	·357 Mag	6	2″	Adjustable
RUGER US					
GP100	Blue or Stainless	·357 Mag	Six	4″ & 6″	Adjustable
Redhawk	Blue or Stainless	·41 Mag, ·44 Mag	Six	5½″ & 7½″	Adjustable
Super Redhawk	Stainless	·44 Mag	Six	7½″ & 9½″	Adjustable

■ *Rossi Model 971.*

■ *Ruger Super Redhawk*
·44 Magnum.

■ *Smith & Wesson Model 15*
Combat Masterpiece. 6 in barrel,
K frame, ·38 Special

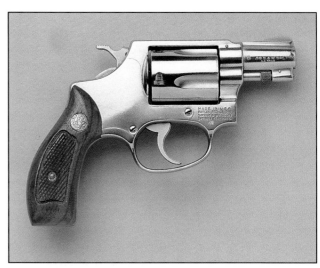

■ *Smith & Wesson Model 60*
Chiefs Special (Stainless). 2 in
barrel, J frame, ·38 Special

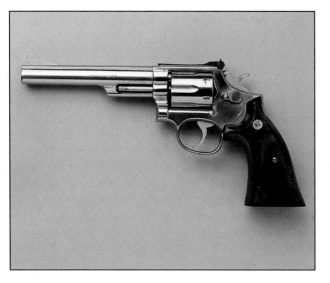

■ *Smith & Wesson Model 66*
Combat Magnum (Stainless). 6 in
barrel, K frame, ·357 Magnum

■ *Smith & Wesson Model 29. 4 in*
barrel, N frame, ·44 Magnum

■ *Smith & Wesson Model 581*
Distinguished Service Magnum.
4 in barrel, L frame ·357
Magnum

DOUBLE ACTION REVOLVERS

SMITH & WESSON US

SMITH & WESSON make a wide range of double action revolvers in a variety of calibres, barrel lengths and finishes. They are all based on four frame sizes, the smallest "J" is for lightweight five shot ·38 and six shot ·22 & ·32 revolvers. The remainder, medium "K" and "L" and large "L" frames are all six shooters. Of the small frames ·38s, the "Bodyguard" models 38, 49 and 649 all have enclosed hammers to facilitate firing from within a pocket. The range and options are tabled for easy reference.

Model	Finish	Calibre	Capacity	Frame	Barrel	Sights
10	Blue, Nickel (4")	·38 Spl	Six	K	2" & 4"	Fixed
13	Blue	·357 Mag	Six	K	3" & 4"	Fixed
15	Blue	·38 Spl	Six	K	2", 4", 6", 8⅜"	Adjustable
17	Blue	·22 LR	Six	K	·4, 6, 8⅜"	Adjustable
19	Blue, Nickel (4" & 6")	·357 Mag	Six	K	2½, 4, 6"	Adjustable
25	Blue	·45 Colt	Six	N	4, 6, 8⅜"	Adjustable
27	Blue	·357 Mag	Six	N	4, 6, 8⅜"	Adjustable
29	Blue, Nkl (ex. 10⅝")	·44 Mag	Six	N	4, 6, 8⅜, 10⅝"	Adjustable
31	Blue	·32 S&W Lo	Six	J	2" & 3"	Fixed
34	Blue	·22 LR	Six	J	2" & 4"	Adjustable
36	Blue, Nickel (2")	·38 Spl	Five	J	2" & 3"	Fixed
37	Blue, Nickel	·38 Spl	Five	J	2"	Fixed
38	Blue, Nickel	·38 Spl	Five	J	2"	Fixed
49	Blue	·38 Spl	Five	J	2"	Fixed
57	Blue	·41 Mag	Six	N	4, 6, 8⅜"	Adjustable
60	Stainless	·38 Spl	Six	J	2"	Fixed
63	Stainless	·22 LR	Six	J	4"	Adjustable
64	Stainless	·38 Spl	Six	K	2, 3, 4"	Fixed
65	Stainless	·357 Mag	Six	K	3" & 4"	Fixed
66	Stainless	·357 Mag	Six	K	2½, 4, 6"	Adjustable
67	Stainless	·38 Spl	Six	K	4"	Adjustable
581	Blue	·357 Mag	Six	L	4"	Fixed
586	Blue, Nickel (4" & 6")	·357 Mag	Six	L	4, 6, 8⅜"	Adjustable
629	Stainless	·44 Mag	Six	N	4, 6, 8⅜"	Adjustable
649	Stainless	·38 Spl	Five	J	2"	Fixed
657	Stainless	·41 Mag	Six	N	4, 6, 8⅜"	Adjustable
681	Stainless	·357 Mag	Six	L	4"	Fixed
686	Stainless	·357 Mag	Six	L	2½, 4, 6, 8⅜"	Adjustable

■ *Smith & Wesson Model 38*
Bodyguard Airweight. 2 in barrel,
J frame, ·38 Special

■ *Smith & Wesson Model 10*
Military & Police. 2 in barrel,
K frame, ·38 Special

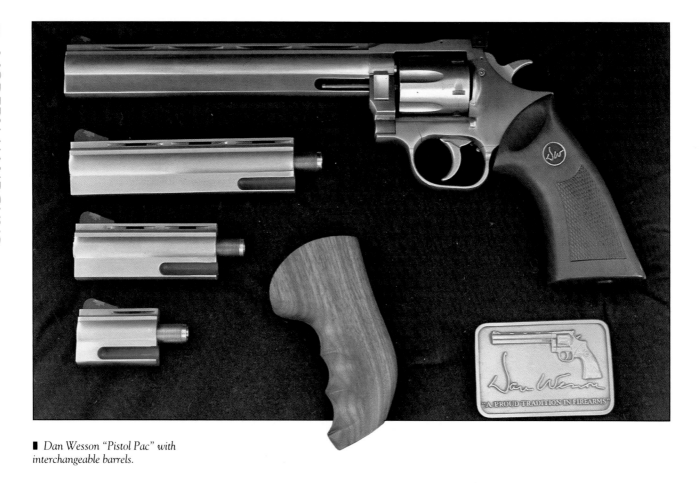

■ *Dan Wesson "Pistol Pac" with interchangeable barrels.*

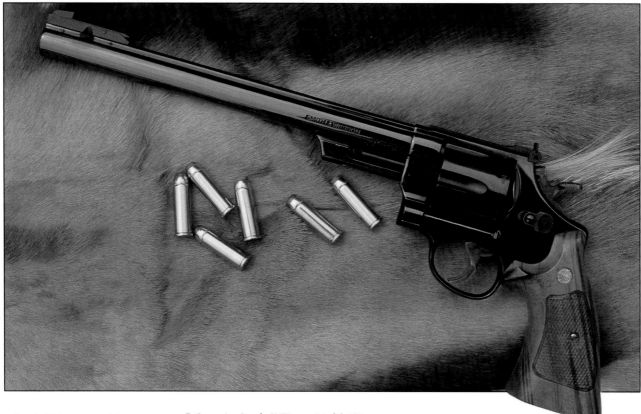

■ *Smith & Wesson Model 29 ·44 Magnum with 10⅝ in barrel and adjustable foresight.*

■ ***Opposite*** *Smith & Wesson Model 657 (Stainless). 3 in barrel, N frame ·41 Magnum (limited edition).*

DOUBLE ACTION REVOLVERS

Model	Calibre(s)	Capacity	Barrel length(s)	Sights	Finish
TAURUS BRAZIL					
65	·357 Mag	Six	3", 4"	Fixed	Blue, Satin Nickel
66 & 669	·357 Mag	Six	3", 4", 6" (66), 4" & 6" fully shrouded (669)	Adjustable	Blue, Satin Nickel (66 only), Stainless
73	·32 S&W Lo (73)	Six	3"	Fixed	Blue, Nickel
80	·38 Spl	Six	3", 4"	Fixed	Blue, Nickel
82	·38 Spl	Six	3", 4" (both HB)	Fixed	Blue, Nickel
83	·38 Spl	Six	4" HB	Adjustable	Blue, Nickel
85	·38 Spl	Five	2", 3"	Fixed	Blue, Nickel, Stainless
86	·38 Spl	Six	6"	Adjustable	Blue
94	·22 LR	Nine	3" & 4"	Adjustable	Blue, Satin Nickel
96	·22 LR	Six	6"	Adjustable	Blue
TOZ USSR					
36 & 49	7·62mm Nagent (7·62 Short – 49)	Six	6"	Adjustable	Blue
UBERTI ITALY					
Inspector	·32 S&W Lo, ·38 Spl	Six	3", 4", 6"	Fixed and adjustable (4" & 6")	Blue, Chrome
DAN WESSON US					
DAN WESSON ARMS produce a range of revolvers in popular calibre with the unique feature (for revolvers) of swiftly interchangeable barrels. Apart from the models 8-2 and 14-2/714, all Dan Wesson revolvers have adjustable sights.					
8-2	·38 Spl	Six	2½", 4", 6", 8"	Fixed	Blue, Stainless
9-2	·38 Spl	Six	2½", 4", 6", 8" interchangeable	Adjustable	Blue, Stainless
14-2 & 714	·357 Mag	Six	2½", 4", 6", 8" interchangeable	Fixed	Blue (14-2), Stainless (714)
15-2 & 715	·357 Mag	Six	2½", 4", 6", 8" interchangeable	Adjustable	Blue (15-2), Stainless (715)
22	·22 LR	Six	2½", 4", 6", 8", 10" interchangeable	Adjustable	Blue, Stainless
32M & 732	·32 H&R Mag	Six	2½", 4", 6", 8" interchangeable	Adjustable	Blue (32M), Stainless (732)
375 Supermag	·375 Supermag (·375 Winchester wildcat)	Six	8"	Adjustable	Blue
40 & 740 Silhouette	·357 Maximum	Six	8", 10" interchangeable	Adjustable	Blue (40), Stainless (740)
41V & 741	·41 Mag	Six	4", 6", 8", 10" interchangeable	Adjustable	Blue (41V), Stainless (741)
44V & 744	·44 Mag	Six	4", 6", 8", 10" interchangeable	Adjustable	Blue (44V), Stainless (744)
45 & 745	·45 Colt	Six	4", 6", 8", 10" interchangeable	Adjustable	Blue (45), Stainless (745)
WEIRAUCH WEST GERMANY					
HW		Six			
Arminius Model HW3	·22 LR, ·22 WMR, ·32 S&W Lo	Eight (·22), Seven (·32)	2¾"	Fixed	Blue or Chrome
Arminius Models HW5 & HW5 T	·22 LR, ·22 WMR, ·32 S&W Lo	Eight (·22), Seven (·32)	4"	Fixed HW5, Adjustable HW5 T	Blue or Chrome
Arminius Models HW7 & HW7 T	·22 LR, ·22 WMR, ·32 S&W Lo	Eight (·22), Seven (·32)	6"	Fixed HW7, Adjustable HW7 T	Blue or Chrome
Arminius Model HW7 S	·22 LR	Eight	6" Vent Rib	Adjustable	Blue
Arminius Model HW9	·22 LR	Six	6" Vent Rib	Adjustable	Blue
Arminius Model HW9 ST	·22 LR	Six	6" Heavy barrel	Adjustable	Blue
Arminius Model HW357	·357 Mag	Six	2½", 4", 6"	Fixed	Blue or Chrome
Arminius Model HW357 T	·357 Mag	Six	3", 4", 6" Vent Rib	Adjustable	Blue or Chrome

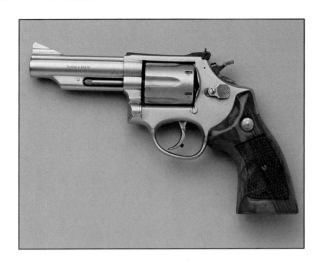

■ *Taurus Model 66 Satin Nickel*
·357 Magnum (handgun illustrated
has a custom trigger stop fitted)

■ ***Above and below*** *Weirauch*
HW357 6-in .357 Magnum

■ *Uberti Inspector 6 in ·38*
Special

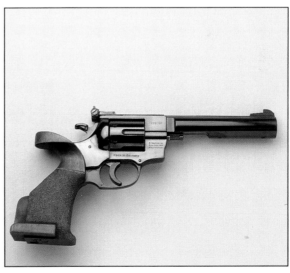

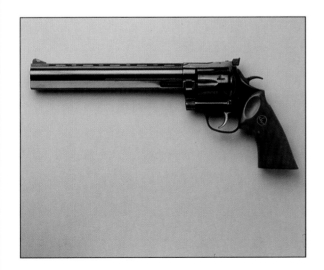

■ *Dan Wesson 44V ·44 Magnum*

DOUBLE ACTION REVOLVERS

Model	Calibre(s)	Capacity	Barrel length(s)	Sights	Finish
Arminius Model HW357 Match	·32 S&W Lo, ·38 Spl, ·357 Mag	Six	6"	Adjustable	Blue
Arminius Model HW38	·38 Spl	Six	2½", 4", 6"	Fixed	Blue or Chrome
Arminius Model HW38T	·38 Spl	Six	3", 4", 6"	Adjustable	Blue or Chrome
Arminius Model HW68 L/Weight	·22LR, ·22 WMR, ·32 S&W Lo	Eight (·22), Seven (·32)	2¾"	Fixed	Black (alloy frame)

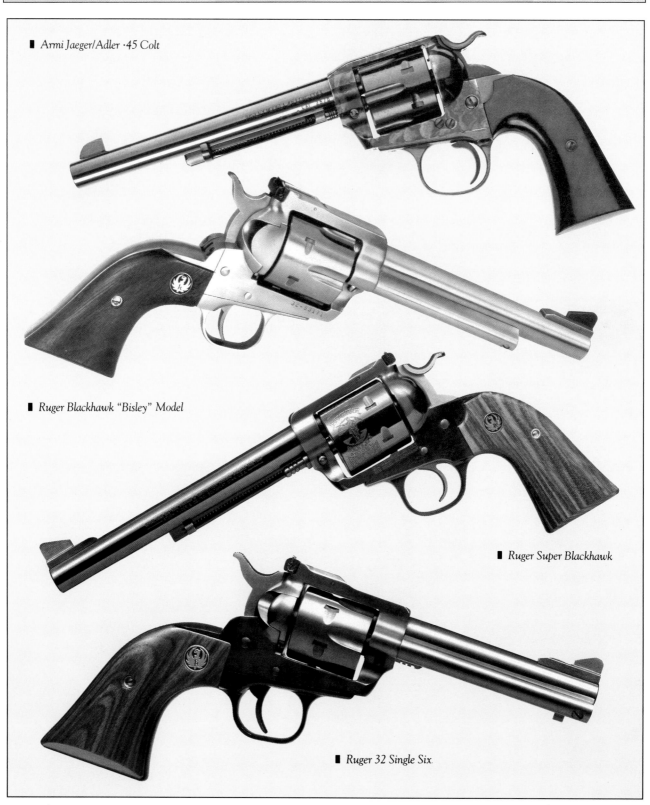

■ Armi Jaeger/Adler ·45 Colt

■ Ruger Blackhawk "Bisley" Model

■ Ruger Super Blackhawk

■ Ruger 32 Single Six

SINGLE ACTION REVOLVERS

Model	Calibre(s)	Capacity	Barrel length(s)	Sights	Finish
ARMI JAEGER ITALY					
Colt Single Action Army	.45 Colt	Six	7½"	Fixed	Blue
CENTURY US					
Model 100	·375 Win, ·444 Marlin, ·45–70	Six	6½", 8", 10", 12"	Adjustable	Manganese bronze frame with blue cylinder and barrel
COLT US					
Single Action Army	·44–40, ·45 Colt	Six	To order	Fixed	To order (Blue or Nickel)
FIE US					
Texas Ranger	·22 LR, ·22 WMR	Six	4¾", 6½", 9"	Fixed	Blue black
FREEDOM ARMS US					
Casull	·454 Casull, ·45 Colt, ·44 Mag	Five	4¾", 6", 7½", 10", 12"	Fixed or adjustable	Stainless
Mini Revolver	·22 LR, ·22 WMR	Five (·22 LR), Four (·22 WMR)	1", 1¾", 3"	Fixed	Stainless
Boot Gun	·22 LR, ·22 WMR	Five (·22 LR) Four (·22 WMR)	3"	Fixed	Stainless
NORTH AMERICAN US					
·450 Magnum Express	·450 Mag Exp, ·45 Win Mag	Five	7½", 10½"	Adjustable	Stainless
Mini-Revolvers	·22 Sh, ·22 LR, ·22 WMR	Five	1⅛" (·22 Sh, ·22 LR), 1⅝" (·22 LR, ·22 WMR), 2½" (·22 WMR)	Fixed	Stainless
PHELPS US					
Heritage I, Eagle I	·444 Marlin, ·45–70 Govt	Six	8", 12"	Adjustable	Blue
RUGER US					
New Model Blackhawk	·30 Carbine, ·357 Mag, ·357 Mag/9mm Lu Convertible, ·41 Mag, ·45 Colt	Six	4⅝" (·357 Mag, ·357 Mag/9mm Lu, ·41 Mag, ·45 Colt), 6½" (·357 Mag, ·357 Mag/9mm Lu, ·41 Mag), 7½" (·30 Carbine, ·45 Colt)	Adjustable	Blue, Stainless (·357 Mag)
New Model Ruger Bisley	·22 LR, ·32 H&R Mag, ·357 Mag, ·41 Mag, ·44 Mag, ·45 Colt	Six	6½" (·22 LR & ·32 Mag), 7½" (·357 Mag – ·45 Colt)	Adjustable windage only	Blue
New Model Super Blackhawk	·44 Mag	Six	5½", 7½", 10½"	Adjustable	Blue, Stainless (7½" & 10½")
New Model Super Single Six	·22 LR/·22 WMR Convertible	Six	4⅝", 5½", 6½", 9½"	Adjustable	Blue, Stainless (5½" & 6½")
New Model ·32 Magnum Single Six	·32 H&R Magnum	Six	4⅝", 5½", 6½", 9½"	Adjustable	Blue
SUPER SIX US					
Golden Bison 45–70 Revolver	·45–70 Gov't	Six	8", 10½"	Adjustable	Manganese bronze frame, antique brown or blue cylinder and barrel
TANARMI ITALY					
TA76	·22 LR, ·22 WMR	Six	4¾"	Adjustable	Blue, Blue & chrome, Chrome
TEXAS LONGHORN US					
Righthand Single Action	"All centrefire pistol calibres"	Six	4¾"	Fixed	Blue, colour case hardened frame
UBERTI ITALY					
1873 Cattleman	·22 LR, ·22 WMR, ·38 Spl, ·357 Mag, ·44–40, ·45 Colt	Six	3" (·44–40 & ·45 Colt), All calibres – 4¾", 5½", 7½"	Fixed, Adjustable	Blue, steel or brass backstrap with colour hardened frame, Stainless
1873 Buckhorn	·44 Mag, ·44 Mag/ ·44–40 Convertible	Six	4¾", 5½", 7½"	Fixed, Adjustable	Blue, steel or brass backstrap with colour hardened frame

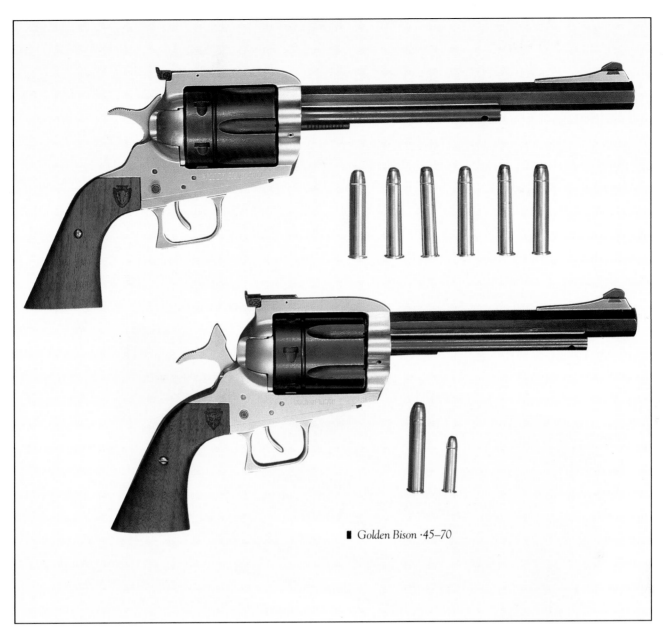

■ *Golden Bison* ·45–70

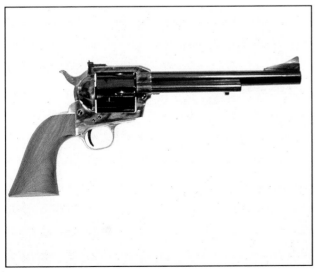

■ *Uberti Cattleman* ·45 Colt

■ *Uberti Phantom* ·357 Magnum

■ *Opposite* Freedom Arms Mini Revolvers
and ·454 Casull

SINGLE ACTION REVOLVERS continued

Model	Calibre(s)	Capacity	Barrel length(s)	Sights	Finish
1873 Buntline	·357 Mag, ·45 Colt, ·44 Mag/·44–40 Convertible	Six	18″	Fixed, Adjustable	Blue, steel or brass backstrap with colour hardened frame
1873 Stallion	·22 LR/·22 WMR Convertible	Six	5½″	Fixed, Adjustable	Blue, steel or brass backstrap with colour hardened frame, Stainless
1875 Army "Outlaw"	·357 Mag, ·44–40, ·45 Colt	Six	7½″	Fixed	Blue with brass trigger guard and colour hardened frame, Nickel
Phantom Silhouette	·357 Mag, ·44 Mag	Six	10½″	Adjustable	Blue
WEIRAUCH WEST GERMANY					
Arminius Models ARM 3575, 445, 455	·357 Mag (3575), ·44 Mag (445), ·45 (455)	Six	5½″	Fixed	Blue, Chrome, Gold, colour hardened frame
ARM 3576 T, 446 T, 456 T	·357 Mag (3576), ·44 Mag (446), ·45 (456)	Six	6″	Adjustable	Blue
ARM 3577, 447, 457	·357 Mag (3577), ·44 Mag (447), ·45 (457)	Six	7½″	Fixed	Blue, Chrome, Gold, colour hardened frame

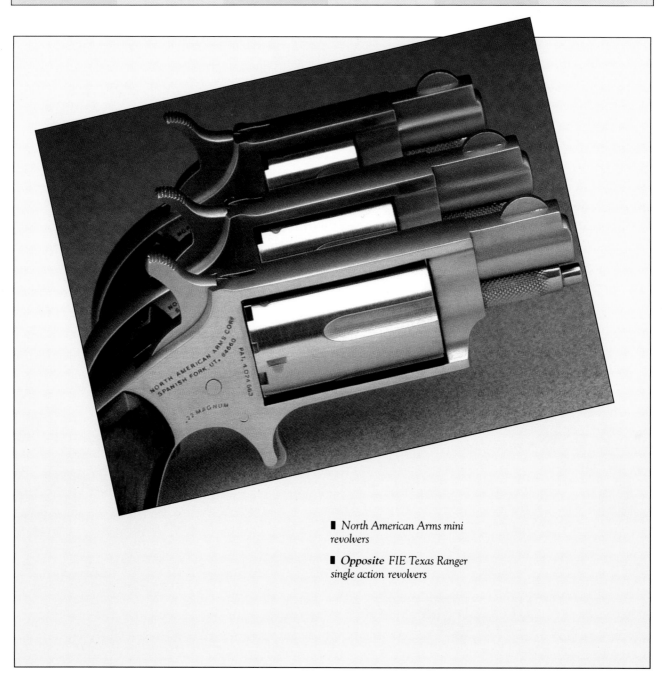

■ *North American Arms mini revolvers*

■ *Opposite* FIE Texas Ranger *single action revolvers*

■ *Top* Browning High
Power "Vigilante"

■ *Above* Davis P32

SELF-LOADING PISTOLS

Self-loading pistols are made by more manufacturers around the world than all other types of handgun put together. Early Luger, Browning and Colt pistols were eagerly adopted for military use after their initial production, but it has taken half a century for them to be generally accepted by police forces and civilians for defensive use. This was partly due to the self-loading pistols' need for good quality ammunition to ensure reliable functioning, and partly to the slightly greater complexity of operation of some self-loaders, with safety catches and magazine releases. No doubt many potential early users of single action self-loading handguns were put off by the need to carry the pistol "cocked and locked" for a rapid first shot, with the fear that the safety catch may slip and an accidental discharge result. Modern double action self-loading pistols have overcome most of these problems and are as safe and reliable to use as double action revolvers, with the added advantage of far greater firepower. New generation 9mm service pistols have magazine capacities of up to 18 rounds of 9mm Luger ammunition compared with the six round cylinder of most revolvers.

In the smaller ·22 LR calibre, many pistols are made for precision target shooting, especially in Europe. Small calibre centrefire pistols are made purely for defence, despite the ineffectiveness of small calibre handguns at stopping an aggressor. In the author's opinion, no pistol cartridge of less power than 9mm Luger is adequate for personal defence, and calibres above ·40 ins (10mm) are preferable.

■ STRAIGHT BLOWBACK

Virtually all modern self-loading handguns of calibres ·380 Auto (9mmK) and below function by straight blowback – the breech block has a powerful spring which holds the cartridge in the chamber as it is fired, the spring alone controlling the movement of the breech and the cycling of the action. Straight blowback makes for simple construction since the barrel can be fixed.

■ BROWNING DELAYED BLOWBACK

In calibres of 9mm Luger and above, some form of delayed blowback is usually needed, since higher pressure cartridges cannot be easily controlled by straight blowback. A very heavy recoil spring would be required, as would a massive breech block to create greater inertia against initial unlocking of the breech.

The most common type of delayed blowback is the Browning type, found in Colt 1911 and Browning GP35 pistols. Both lock lugs on the barrel into grooves in the slide under chamber pressure until the bullet has left the barrel and the pressure starts to drop. As the pressure falls,

■ *Small calibre European self-loading pistols have proved very popular for precision target shooting.* **Top & lower left** *·32 and ·22 versions of the Walther GSP* **Lower right** *Hämmerli 208*

the barrel cams down on a swinging link in Colt 1911 designs, or by a sliding cam in GP35 types. The slide then recoils under the residual pressure controlled by a light recoil spring, cycling the action, cocking the hammer and chambering a fresh round of ammunition. The movement of the barrel during cycling needs adequate clearance of bearing surfaces to ensure reliability under adverse conditions, and this leads to claims of inaccuracy in many service issue pistols. This is not significant at battle pistols' normal operational ranges, but does become noticeable when the same handgun is used for longer range, precision target shooting, and tuning or tightening of actions is needed.

■ OTHER FORMS OF DELAYED BLOWBACK

Heckler & Koch use two alternatives to the Browning locked breech action in their high pressure self-loading pistols. The P9S uses roller locking to delay blowback, with a mechanism derived from their military rifles. The P7 uses a

■ *Screen actor Charles Bronson used a Wildey pistol in Death Wish Three.*

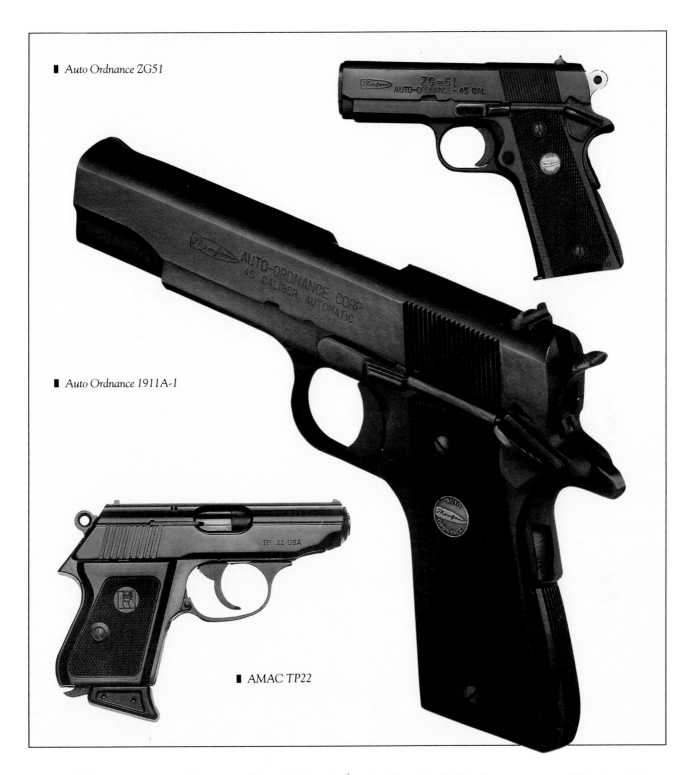

■ *Auto Ordnance ZG51*

■ *Auto Ordnance 1911A-1*

■ AMAC TP22

gas-retarded system using propellant gas to keep the breech locked up until the pressure drops; it then acts as straight blowback pistol with a fixed barrel. The high gas pressure ensures that the P7 will function without an extractor if necessary, the spent case being blown out of the chamber. Steyr uses an annular gas ring around the barrel to accomplish delayed blowback in its high magazine capacity GB pistol.

■ GAS OPERATION

Gas operation is more complex, requiring a gas piston and heavy spring to control blowback. Gas operated pistols are usually bulky, best suited to very powerful calibres, but use a fixed barrel, which enhances accuracy. The Auto Mag in ·44 and ·357 AMP was one of the first moderately successful self-loading pistols, but it was not popular due to the lack of commercially-made ammunition. AMT still make a ·22 WMR version of the Auto Mag. The Wildey pistols in ·45 Win Mag and 9mm Win Mag have been a more successful attempt to create a big bore gas-operated self-loader. More recently, the Israeli Desert Eagle has become available using high pressure ·357 Magnum and ·44 Magnum revolver ammunition. Gas-operated self-loaders generally require good quality, high powered ammunition for reliable functioning.

SELF LOADING PISTOLS

Model	Calibre(s)	Type of action	Capacity	Barrel length(s)	Sights	Finish
AMAC US						
TP–22	·22 LR, ·25 Auto	Blowback	Seven	2·8"	Fixed	Blue
AMT US						
Automag II	·22 WMR	Gas assisted	Ten	6"	Adjustable	Stainless
Backup	·22 LR, ·380 Auto/ 9mmK	Blowback	Eight (·22 LR), Five (·380)	2½"	Fixed	Stainless
Hardballer & Government Models	·45 ACP	Delayed blowback	Seven	5"	Adjustable (Hardballer) Fixed (Gov't)	Stainless
Hardballer Longslide	·45 ACP	Delayed blowback	Seven	7"	Adjustable	Stainless
Lightning	·22 LR	Blowback	Ten	5", 6½", 8½", 10"	Adjustable	Stainless
AMERICAN ARMS US						
Eagle 380	·380 Auto/9mmK	Blowback	Six	2½"	Fixed	Stainless, Oxide, Teflon
ARMINEX US						
Sleeping Beauty	·380 Auto/9mmK	Blowback			Fixed	
ASTRA SPAIN						
A-60	·380 Auto/9mmK	Blowback, Double action	Thirteen	3½"	Fixed	Blue
A-90	9mm Luger, ·45 ACP	Delayed blowback, Double action	Fifteen (9mm), Nine (·45 ACP)	3¾"	Fixed	Blue
Constable	·22 LR, ·380 Auto/ 9mmK	Blowback, Double action	Ten (·22 LR), Seven (·380 Auto/9mmK)	3½"	Fixed	Blue, Stainless, Chrome
AUTO ORDNANCE US						
1911A-1	9mm Luger, ·38 Super, ·45 ACP	Colt delayed blowback	Seven	5"	Fixed	Blue
ZG51	·45 ACP	Colt delayed blowback	Six	3½"	Fixed	Blue
BENELLI ITALY						
B76	9mm Luger	Delayed blowback, Double action	Eight	4¼"	Fixed	Blue
BERNADELLI ITALY						
PO18 DA	9mm Luger	Delayed blowback, Double action	Sixteen	4.8"	Fixed	Blue
PO18 Combat	9mm Luger	Delayed blowback, Double action	Fourteen	4.1"	Fixed	Blue
Models 60, 80, 90	·22 LR, ·32 Auto (7·65mm), ·380 Auto/ 9mmK (60 & 90 only)	Blowback	Ten (·22 LR), Nine (·32 Auto), Seven (·380 Auto/9mmK)	3½", 6" (Model 90)	Adjustable	Blue
BERETTA ITALY						
Model 21	·22 LR	Blowback, Double action	Seven	2½"	Fixed	Blue
Models 81BB, 84BB, 82BB, 85BB, 87BB	·32 Auto/7·65mmBr (81 & 82), ·380 Auto/ 9mmK (84 & 85), ·22 LR (87)	Blowback, Double action	Thirteen (84), twelve (81), nine (82), eight (85 & 87)	3¾"	Fixed	Blue
Models 92F, 92F Compact & 98F	9mm Luger (92F & 92F Compact), 9 × 21mm (98F), ·30 Luger/7·65 Para (98F)	Delayed blowback, Double action	Fifteen (92F & 98F), thirteen (92F Compact)	4·92" (92F & 98F), 4·3" (92F Compact)	Fixed	Blue
Model 93R	9mm Luger	Delayed blowback, Double action, Burst fire capability	Twenty	6·14"	Fixed	Blue
950 BS	·22 Short, ·25 Auto (6·35mm)	Blowback, Double action	Seven (·22 Sh), Nine (·25 Auto)	2½", 4" (·22 Sh)	Fixed	Blue
BERSA ARGENTINA						
Models 223DA, 224, 226	·22 LR	Blowback	Eleven	3½" (223), 4" (224), 6" (226)	Adjustable windage	Blue
Model 383	·380 Auto/9mmK	Blowback	Nine	3½"	Adjustable windage	Blue
BRNO CZECHOSLOVAKIA						
Models CZ75 & CZ85	9mm Luger	Delayed blowback, Double action	Fifteen	4.7"	Adjustable windage	Blue
CZ83	·32 Auto/7·65mm, ·380 Auto/9mmK	Blowback, Double action	Fifteen (·32), thirteen (·380)	3·7"	Adjustable windage	Blue

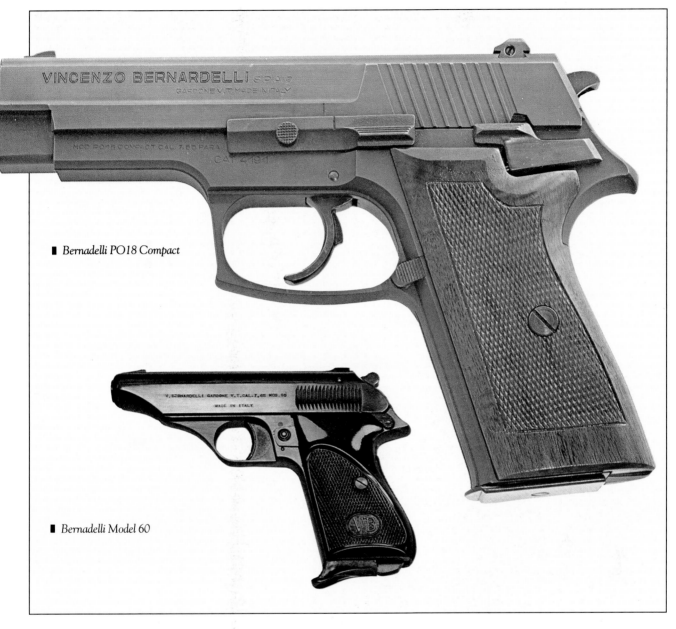

■ *Bernadelli PO18 Compact*

■ *Bernadelli Model 60*

■ *Beretta Model 81*

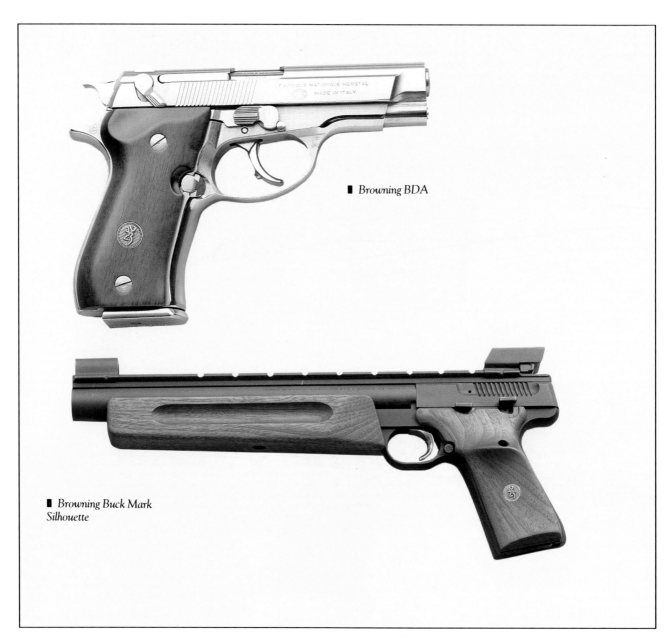

■ *Browning BDA*

■ *Browning Buck Mark Silhouette*

■ *Browning Buck Mark*

■ *Right* BRNO CZ 83.

■ *Below left* Caspian ·45 pistol (illustrated fitted with British CD Compensator system).

■ *Below right* Colt Combat Commander.

■ *Bottom* Colt Delta Elite 10mm.

SELF LOADING PISTOLS continued

Model	Calibre(s)	Type of action	Capacity	Barrel length(s)	Sights	Finish
BROWNING ITALY						
BDA	·380 Auto/9mmK	Blue, Double action	Thirteen	3¾"	Fixed	Blue
BROWNING US						
Buck Mark 22	·22 LR	Blowback	Ten	5½"	Adjustable	Blue
Models Buck Mark Silhouette & Buck Mark Varmint	·22 LR	Blowback	Ten	9⅞"	Adjustable (Silhouette), None – scope rail (Varmint)	Blue
BROWNING BELGIUM						
Models International & Practice 150 Target Pistols	·22 LR	Blowback	Ten	6¾"	Adjustable	Blue
Hi-Power Models Vigilante, MkII, Sport, Competition Target Pistol	9mm Luger	Browning delayed blowback	Thirteen	4·66" – all mods except Competition 5·9"	Fixed (Vigilante & MkII), Adjustable (Sport & Competition)	Blue
BUMBLE BEE US						
Pocket Partner	·22 LR	Blowback	Eight	2¼"	Fixed	Blue
CASPIAN ARMS US						
Combat Competition	·45 ACP	Colt delayed blowback	Seven	5"	Adjustable	Stainless
COLT US						
Combat Commander	9mm Luger, ·38 Super, ·45 ACP	Delayed blowback	Nine (9mm & ·38 Sup), Seven (·45 ACP)	4¼"	Fixed	Blue
Combat Elite	·45 ACP	Delayed blowback	Seven	5"	Fixed	Stainless frame, blue slide
Delta Elite	10mm Auto	Delayed blowback	Seven	5"	Fixed	Blue
Gold Cup National Match Target Pistol	·45 ACP	Delayed blowback	Seven	5"	Adjustable	Blue, Stainless
Government MkIV/Series 80	9mm Luger, ·38 Super, ·45 ACP	Delayed blowback	Nine (9mm & ·38 Sup), Seven (·45 ACP)	5"	Fixed	Blue (all), Stainless (·45 ACP only)
Officers ACP	·45 ACP	Delayed blowback	Six	3½"	Fixed	Blue, Stainless
380 Government	·380 Auto/9mmK	Delayed blowback	Seven	3¼"	Fixed	Blue, Nickel
Models Mustang 380 & Mustang Pocket Lite, Mustang Plus II	·380 Auto/9mmK	Delayed blowback	Five (Mustang 380 & Pocket Lite), Seven (Mustang Plus II)	2¾"	Fixed	Blue, Nickel
COONAN ARMS US						
·357 Magnum Auto Pistol	·357 Magnum	Delayed blowback	Seven	5"	Adjustable windage. Fully adjustable to order	Stainless
DAVIS US						
P–32	·32 Auto/7·65mm	Blowback	Six	2·8"	Fixed	Black Teflon or Chrome
DETONICS US						
Combat Master Models MkI & MkVI	·45 ACP	Delayed blowback	Six	3½"	Fixed (MkI), Adjustable (MkVI)	Stainless
Servicemaster	·45 ACP	Delayed blowback	Seven	4¼"	Fixed	Stainless
Scoremaster	·45 ACP, ·451 Detonics Magnum	Delayed blowback	Seven	4½", 5", 6"	Adjustable	Stainless
ERMA WEST GERMANY						
EP 752	·22 LR	Blowback	Eight	3¼"	Fixed	Blue
KPG22	·22 LR	Luger type toggle	Eight	4"	Fixed	Blue
FAS ITALY						
601 Rapid Fire Target Pistol	·22 Short	Blowback	Five	5·6"	Adjustable	Blue

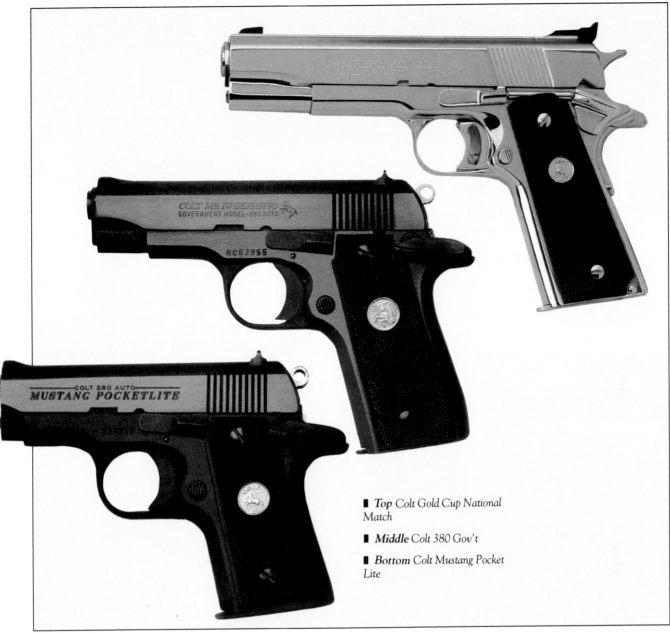

■ **Top** Colt Gold Cup National Match

■ **Middle** Colt 380 Gov't

■ **Bottom** Colt Mustang Pocket Lite

■ Colt Officers ACP

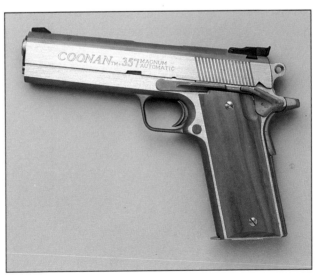

■ Coonan ·357 Magnum Automatic

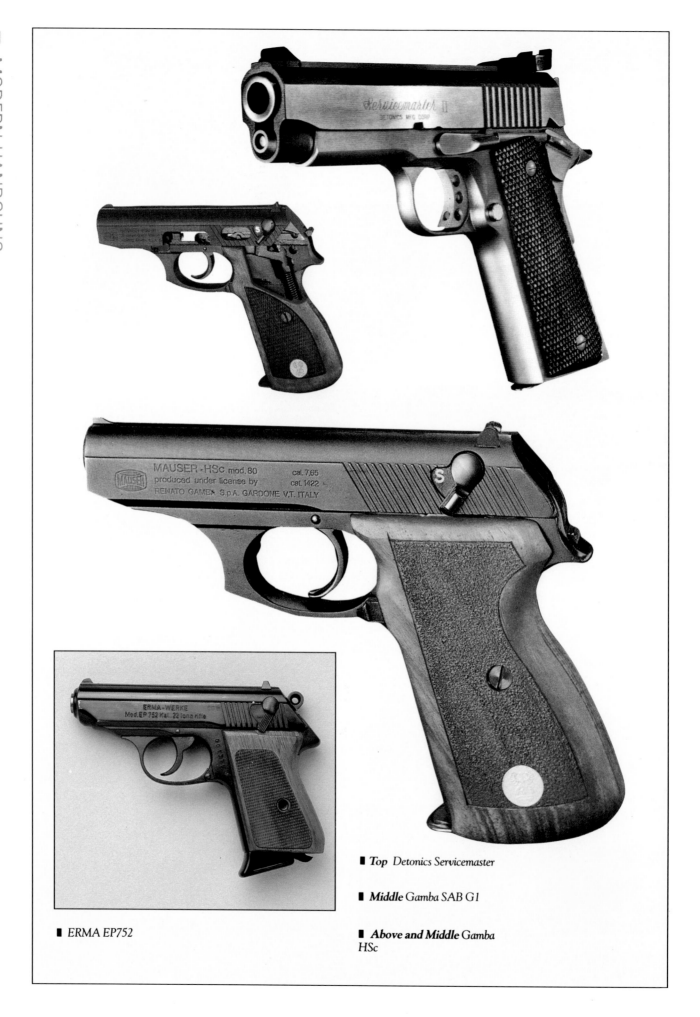

■ **Top** Detonics Servicemaster

■ **Middle** Gamba SAB G1

■ **Above and Middle** Gamba HSc

■ ERMA EP752

■ *Top* Grendel P-10

■ *Right* Glock 17

SELF LOADING PISTOLS continued

Model	Calibre(s)	Type of action	Capacity	Barrel length(s)	Sights	Finish
602 Target Pistol	·22 LR	Blowback	Five	5·6″	Adjustable	Blue
·32 Target Pistol	·32 S&W Long Wadcutter	Blowback	Five		Adjustable	Blue
FEDERAL ORDNANCE US						
Ranger	·45 ACP	Colt delayed blowback	Seven	5″	Fixed	Stainless
FEG HUNGARY						
FP9	9mm Luger	Delayed blowback	Fourteen	4·675″	Fixed	Blue
P9R	9mm Luger	Delayed blowback, double action	Fourteen	4·675″	Fixed	Blue
PPH	·32 Auto/7·65mm & ·380 Auto/9mmK	Blowback, double action	Seven	3·86″	Fixed	Alloy frame, blue steel slide
GAMBA ITALY						
HSc80	·32 Auto/7·65mm, ·380 Auto/9mmK, 9mm Ultra/9 × 18mm	Blowback, double action	Fifteen	3·34″	Fixed	Blue
Models SAB "G" 90 & SAB "G" 91 Compact	·30/7·65mm Luger, 9mm Ultra/9 × 18mm, 9 × 21mm	Delayed blowback, double action	Fifteen, Twelve (Compact)	4·72″, 3·5″ (Compact)	Fixed	Blue
GLOCK AUSTRIA						
Models 17, 19 Compact, 17L Competition	9mm Luger	Locked breech recoil operated, double action	Seventeen (17 & 17L), Fifteen (19 Compact)	4·48″ (17), 6″ ported (17L), 4″ Compact	Adjustable	Polymer frame, blue steel slide
GÖNCZ US						
High-Tech Long Pistol Models GA, GS, GAT	·30/7·63 Mauser, ·38 Super, 9mm Luger, ·45 ACP	Closed bolt blowback	Eighteen & thirty-two (·30/7·63 Mauser, ·38 Super, 9mm Luger), ten and twenty (·45 ACP)	4″, 9½″	Adjustable	Matte black oxide and anodised
GRENDEL US						
P-10	·380 Auto/9mmK	Blowback, trigger cocked only, integral magazine	Ten	3″	Fixed	Polycarbonate grip and trigger guard, black oxide frame and slide
HÄMMERLI SWITZERLAND						
Models 208, 211 & 215 Target Pistols	·22 LR	Blowback	Eight	5·9″	Adjustable	Blue
212 Hunters Pistol	·22 LR	Blowback	Eight	4·88″	Adjustable windage	Blue
280	·22 LR, ·32 S&W Long Wadcutter	Blowback	Six (·22 LR), Five (·32)	4·58″	Adjustable	Black carbon fibre frame and barrel shroud, black steel slide
232 Rapid Fire Target Pistol	·22 Short	Blowback, vented barrel	Five	5·2″	Adjustable	Blue
HECKLER & KOCH WEST GERMANY						
Models P7K3	·22 LR, ·32 Auto/7·65mm, ·380 Auto/9mmK	Blowback, squeeze cocked	Eight	4·13″	Fixed	Blue
Models P7-M8 & P7-M13	9mm Luger	Gas retarded blowback, squeeze cocked	Eight (–M8), thirteen (–M13)	4·13″	Fixed	Blue
P9S	9mm Luger, ·45 ACP	Roller locked delayed blowback, double action	Nine (9mm Luger), Seven (·45 ACP)	4″	Fixed	Blue
VP70 & VP70Z	9mm Luger	Trigger cocked – semi automatic (VP70Z) with burst fire capability (VP70 only)	Eighteen	4·56″	Fixed	Blue
INTERARMS US (under licence from West Germany)						
Walther PPK	·380 Auto/9mmK	Blowback	Six	3·27″	Fixed	Blue, Stainless
Walther TPH	·22 LR	Blowback	Six	2¼″	Fixed	Stainless

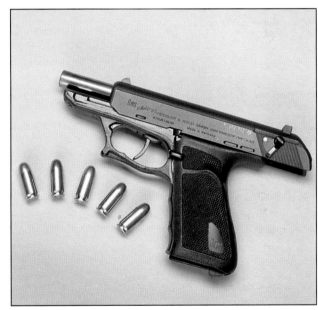

■ *Top* Heckler & Koch P7M13

■ *Above left & right* Heckler & Koch P9S

■ *Left* Heckler & Koch VP70 Z

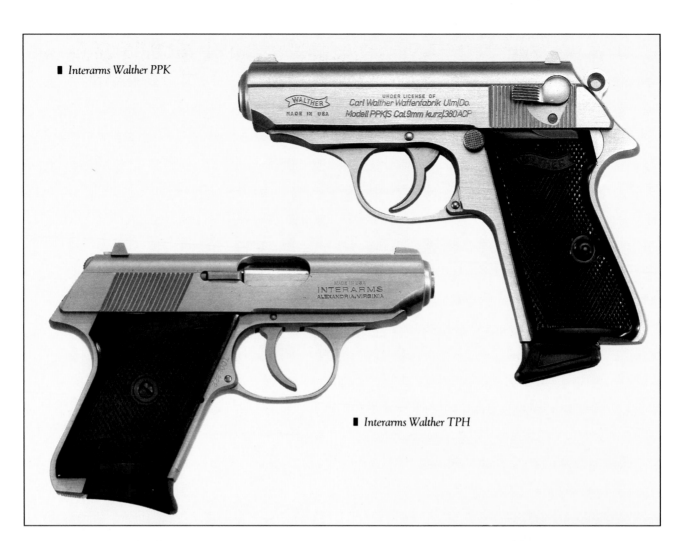

■ *Interarms Walther PPK*

■ *Interarms Walther TPH*

Above IMI Desert Eagle

■ ***Right*** LAR Grizzly

■ *ITM AT 84S*

90

SELF LOADING PISTOLS continued

Model	Calibre(s)	Type of action	Capacity	Barrel length(s)	Sights	Finish
ISRAEL MILITARY INDUSTRIES ISRAEL						
Desert Eagle	·357 Magnum, ·44 Magnum	Gas operated	Nine (·357), Eight (·44)	6", 10", 14" interchangeable	Adjustable windage	Black epoxy, Stainless frame, Alloy frame
ITM SWITZERLAND						
AT 84	9mm Luger, ·41 Action Express	Delayed blowback, double action	Fifteen (9mm)	4·72"	Fixed	Blue
JENNINGS US						
J-22	·22 LR	Blowback	Six	2½"	Fixed	Chrome, Nickel, Black Teflon
KORRIPHILA WEST GERMANY						
HSP 701	9mm Luger, ·38 Spl Wadcutter, ·38 Super, ·45 ACP	Roller locked (Budichowsky) delayed blowback, double action	Nine (9mm Luger), Seven (·45 ACP)	4", 5"	Adjustable	Blue
KORTH WEST GERMANY						
Pistol	9mm Luger, 9 × 21mm	Delayed blowback	Thirteen	4"	Adjustable	Blue
LAR US						
Grizzly	·45 Win Mag, ·357 Mag, 10mm Auto, ·45 ACP	Delayed blowback	Seven	5·4", 6·5"	Adjustable	Blue, Hard Chrome
LLAMA SPAIN						
IX-A & XI-B	·45 ACP (IX-A), 9mm Luger (XI-B)	Delayed blowback	Seven (·45 ACP), Nine (9mm Luger)	5", 4·31"	Fixed	Blue
Omni	9mm Luger, ·45 ACP	Delayed blowback, double action	Seven (·45 ACP), Nine (9mm Luger)	4·31"	Fixed	Blue
Small frame pistols	·22 LR, ·32 Auto/7·65mm, ·380 Auto/9mmK	Blowback (·22 & 32), Delayed blowback (·380 Auto/9mmK)	Seven (·32)	3¾"	Fixed	Blue
MAKAROV USSR & EAST GERMANY						
Makarov	9mm Makarov	Double action, straight blowback	Eight	3·7"	Fixed	Blue
MAS FRANCE						
GI Beretta 92F copy	9mm Luger	Delayed blowback, double action	Fifteen	4·92"	Fixed	Blue
MAUSER WEST GERMANY						
Parabellum '08 "Luger" replica	·30/7·65mm Luger, 9mm Luger	Blowback, toggle locked	Eight	4"	Fixed	Blue and highly engraved special order models
MORINI SWITZERLAND						
CM100, CM102E	·22 LR	Blowback, tubular magazine (electronic trigger on 102E)	Five	6"	Adjustable	Blue
CM120, CM122E Rapid fire pistol	·22 Short	Blowback, tubular magazine (electronic trigger on 122E)	Seven	5½"	Adjustable	Blue
CM140, CM142E	·32 S&W Lo-WC	Blowback, tubular magazine (electronic trigger on 142E)	Five	6"	Adjustable	Blue
MKE TURKEY						
Krikkale	·380 Auto/9mmK	Blowback, double action	Seven	4"	Adjustable	Blue
NAVY ARMS US						
Standard Luger	·22 LR	Blowback Luger type toggle action	Ten	4"	Fixed	Blue
NORINCO CHINA						
Type 54	7·62mm Tokarev	Single action locked breech blowback	Eight	4·6"	Fixed	Blue
Type 59	9mm Makarov	Double action, straight blowback	Eight	3·7"	Fixed	Blue
Type 64	7·62 × 17mm Chinese	Double action blowback	Seven	3·4"	Fixed	Blue

■ *Llama large frame ·45 & small frame ·32 autos*

■ **Left** Smith & Wesson 645

■ **Below** Tanfoglio TA90

■ **Above and left** *Makarov*

■ *Browning Buck Mark Plus*

■ *Wilkinson Sherry*

■ *Steel City War Eagle (**top**)
and Double Deuce*

■ *Heckler & Koch P7M8*

SELF LOADING PISTOLS continued

Model	Calibre(s)	Type of action	Capacity	Barrel length(s)	Sights	Finish
Type 77	7·62 × 17mm Chinese	Single action blowback	Seven	3·4"	Fixed	Blue
BS-01 Target pistol	·22 LR	Blowback	Six	6"	Adjustable	Blue
PS-01 Target pistol	·22 LR	Blowback	Ten	7·1"	Adjustable	Blue
SS-01 Rapid fire target pistol	·22 Sh	Blowback	Six	6·6"	Adjustable	Blue
OLIMPIC SPAIN						
Rapid fire target pistol	·22 Short	Blowback	Five	5"	Adjustable	Blue
RAVEN ARMS US						
MP-25	·25 Auto/6·35mm	Blue	Six	2·44"	Fixed	Blue, Nickel, Chrome
RUGER US						
Mark II	·22 LR	Blue	Ten	4¾" & 6" (Standard Model), 6⅞" (Target Model), 5½", 6⅞", 10" (Bull Barrel Model)	Adjustable windage (Standard model), Adjustable (all others)	Blue, Stainless
P85	9mm Luger	Delayed blowback, double action	Fifteen	4½"	Fixed	Blue
SAKO FINLAND						
Triace Target pistol	·22 Short, ·22 LR, ·32 S&W Long Wadcutter	Blowback	Six	5·9"	Adjustable	Blue
SARDIUS ISRAEL						
SD-9	9mm Luger	Blowback, double action	Seven	3"	Fixed	Parkerized pressed steel
SEECAMP US						
LWS 32	·25 Auto/6·35mm, ·32 Auto/7·65mm	Blowback, trigger cocked only	Six	2"	None	Stainless
SIG SWITZERLAND						
P210 Models 1, 2, 5, 6	·30/7·65mm Luger, 9mm Luger	Delayed blowback	Eight	4·72"/120mm (Models 1, 2, 6), 5·9"/150mm (Model 5)	Fixed (Models 1 & 2), Adjustable (Models 5 & 6)	Blue
SIG-SAUER WEST GERMANY						
P-220	9mm Luger, ·38 Super, ·45 ACP	Delayed blowback, double action	Nine (9mm Luger & ·38 Super), Seven (·45 ACP)	4⅜"	Fixed	Blue
P-225	9mm Luger	Delayed blowback, double action	Eight	3·8"	Fixed	Blue
P-226	9mm Luger	Delayed blowback, double action	Fifteen	4·4"	Fixed	Blue, Nickel, Polymer finish
P230	·32 Auto/7·65mm, ·380 Auto/9mmK	Blowback, double action	Eight (·32 Auto/7·65mm), Seven (·380 Auto/9mmK)	3¾"	Fixed	Blue, Stainless

SMITH & WESSON US

SMITH & WESSON manufactures a far smaller range of self-loading pistols compared with its revolver selection, but still gives one of the widest choices of pistol types in four calibres.

Model	Calibre	Action	Trigger	Capacity	Barrel	Sights	Finish
41	·22 LR	B/back	SA	10	5½"	Adj	Blue
52	·38 Spl-WC	D/b-bk	SA	5	5"	Adj	Blue
422	·22 LR	B/Back	SA	10	4½" & 6"	Adj/Fix	Blue
439	9mm Luger	D/b-bk	DA	8	4"	Adj	Blue
459	9mm Luger	D/b-bk	DA	14	4"	Adj	Blue
469	9mm Luger	D/b-bk	DA	12	3½"	Adj	Blue
639	9mm Luger	D/b-bk	DA	8	4"	Adj	Stainless
645	·45 ACP	D/b-bk	DA	8	5"	Adj	Stainless
659	9mm Luger	D/b-bk	DA	14	4"	Adj	Stainless
669	9mm Luger	D/b-bk	DA	12	3½"	Adj	Stainless
745	·45 ACP	D/b-bk	SA	8	5"	Fixed	Stainless

■ *Ruger Mk II*

■ *Ruger P85*

■ *Sako Triace*

■ *SIG-Sauer P226*

■ *Smith & Wesson Model 52*

■ *Smith & Wesson Model 669*

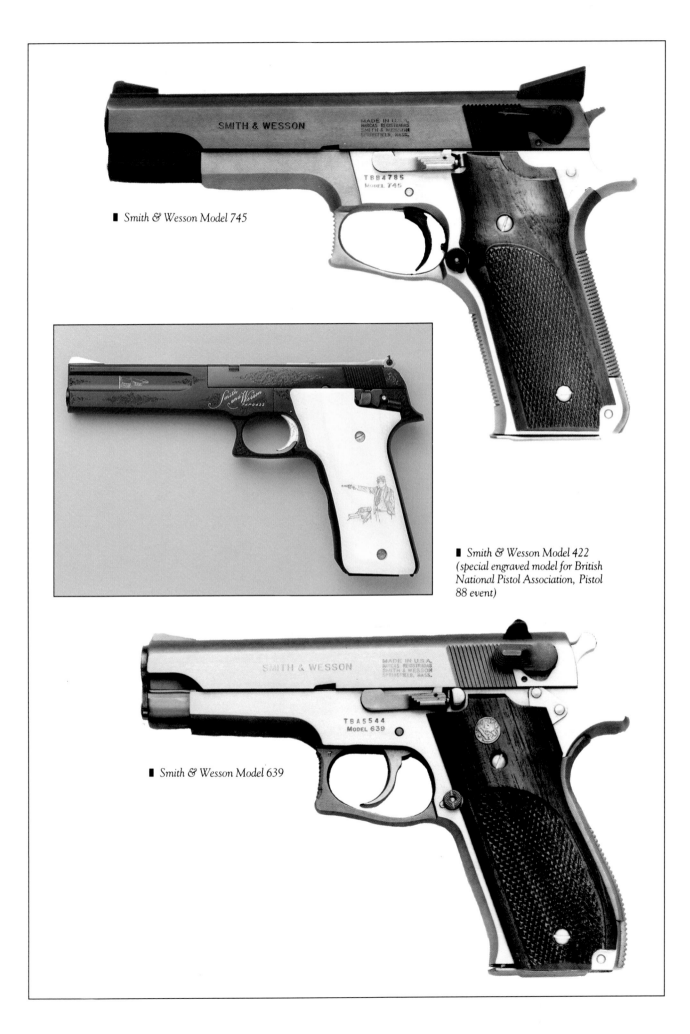

■ *Smith & Wesson Model 745*

■ *Smith & Wesson Model 422*
(special engraved model for British National Pistol Association, Pistol 88 event)

■ *Smith & Wesson Model 639*

SELF LOADING PISTOLS continued

Model	Calibre(s)	Type of action	Capacity	Barrel length(s)	Sights	Finish
SOKOLOVSKY US						
45 Automaster	·45 ACP	Delayed blowback	Six	6"	Adjustable	Stainless
SPRINGFIELD ARMOURY US						
1911-A1	·38 Super, 9mm Luger, ·45 ACP	Delayed blowback	Nine (·38 Super, 9mm Luger), Eight (·45 ACP)	5"	Fixed	Blue, Parkerized
SPRINGFIELD ARMOURY US – Frame/WEST GERMANY – Slide and barrel						
Omega	·38 Spl-WC, ·38 Super, 9mm Luger, 10mm Auto, ·45 ACP	Delayed blowback	Nine (·38 Super, 9mm Luger), Eight (·45 ACP)	5", 6"	Adjustable	Blue
STAR SPAIN						
Models 30M & 30PK	9mm Luger	Delayed blowback, double action	Fifteen	4·3" (Model M), 3·86" (Model PK)	Adjustable	Blue
Models BM & BKM	9mm Luger	Delayed blowback	Eight	3·9"	Fixed	Blue, Chrome (BM only)
PD	·45 ACP	Delayed blowback	Six	3·94"	Adjustable	Blue
STEEL CITY US						
Double Deuce	·22 LR, ·25 Auto/6·35mm	Blowback	Seven (·22 LR), Six (·25 Auto)	2½"	Fixed	Stainless
War Eagle	9mm Luger	Delayed blowback, double action	Fifteen	4", 6"	Fixed, Adjustable	Stainless
STEYR AUSTRIA						
GB	9mm Luger	Gas retarded blowback, double action	Eighteen	5·39"	Fixed	Blue
F TANFOGLIO ITALY						
TA90	9mm Luger	Delayed blowback, double action	Fifteen	4·7"	Fixed	Blue
G TANFOGLIO ITALY						
GT27	·25 Auto/6·35 mm	Blowback	Six	2·48"	Fixed	Blue, Chrome
Models GT32 & GT380	·32 Auto/7·65mm (GT32), ·380 Auto/9mmK (GT380)	Blowback	Six	4⅞"	Fixed	Blue, Chrome
GT380XE	·380 Auto/9mmK	Blowback	Eleven	3·88"	Fixed	Blue, Satin nickel
TAURUS BRAZIL						
Models PT-92 AF & PT-99 AF	9mm Luger	Delayed blowback, double action	Fifteen	4·92"	Fixed (Model 92), Adjustable (Model 99)	Blue, Satin Nickel
PT 58	·380 Auto/9mmK	Blowback, double action	Thirteen	3¾"	Fixed	Blue, Satin Nickel
UNIQUE FRANCE						
DES 32 Target pistol	·32 S&W Long Wadcutter	Blowback	Five	5·91"	Adjustable	Blue
DES 69 Target pistol	·22 LR	Blowback	Five	5·91"	Adjustable	Blue
DES/823 U Rapid fire target pistol	·22 Short	Blowback	Five	5·91"	Adjustable	Blue
VICTORY ARMS ENGLAND						
MC5	9mm Luger, ·38 Super, ·41 Action Express, ·45 ACP (interchangeable)	Locked breech delayed blowback, double action	Seventeen (9mm Luger & 38 Super), Twelve (·41 AE), Ten (·45 ACP)	4⅜", 5⅞", 7½" interchangeable	Adjustable windage	Blue
WALTHER WEST GERMANY						
Models GSP & GSP-MV Target pistols	·22 LR & ·32 S&W Long Wadcutter (interchangeable)	Blowback	Five	5·3" (·22 LR), 4·21" (·32 S&W Lo)	Adjustable	Blue (GSP), Satin Nickel (GSP-MV)
GSP-Junior Target pistol	·22 LR	Blowback	Five	4·21"	Adjustable	Blue
OSP Rapid fire target pistol	·22 Short	Blowback	Five	4·25"	Adjustable	Blue
P5	·32 Auto/7·65mm, 9mm Luger	Delayed blowback (9mm), blowback (·32), double action	Eight	3½"	Adjustable windage	Blue
P5 Compact	9mm Luger	Delayed blowback, double action	Eight	3"	Adjustable windage	Blue

■ *Sokolovsky Automaster*

■ ***Above and left*** *Springfield Armoury 1911 Defender and Combat Commander*

■ **Above** Star 30 M

■ *Springfield Armoury "Omega"*
5 in and 6 in Models

■ **Opposite** top Star BM

■ **Opposite** bottom Star PD

102

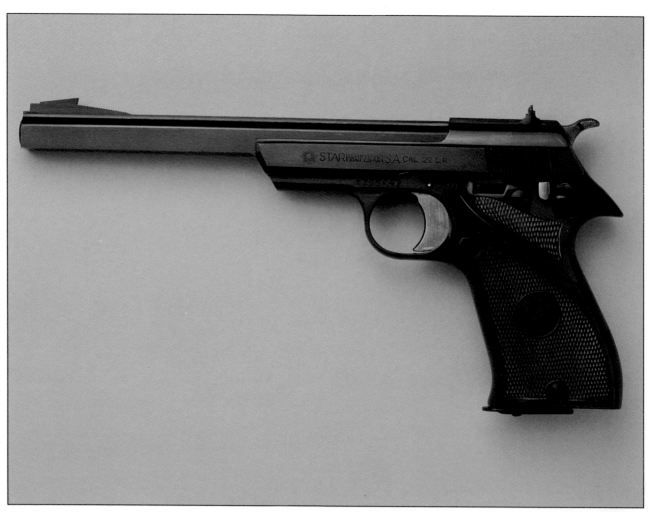

■ *Top* Star FR

■ *Right* Star 30 BK

▌ **Top** *Taurus PT99*

▌ **Below** *Victory Arms MC5*

▌ **Right** *Walther GSP*

SELF LOADING PISTOLS continued

Model	Calibre(s)	Type of action	Capacity	Barrel length(s)	Sights	Finish
P38	9mm Luger	Delayed blowback, double action	Eight	4·94″	Fixed	Blue
P88	9mm Luger	Delayed blowback, double action	Fifteen	4″	Adjustable	Blue
PP	·22 LR, ·32 Auto/ 7·65mm, ·380 Auto, 9mmK	Blowback, double action	Eight (·22 & ·32), Seven (·380)	3·86″	Fixed	Blue
PPK & PPK-S	·32 Auto/7·65mm, ·380 Auto,9mmK	Blowback, double action	Seven (·32), Six (·380)	3·27″	Fixed	Blue (PPK), Stainless (PPK-S)
TPH	·22 LR, ·25 Auto/ 6·35mm	Blowback, double action	Six	2¼″	Fixed	Blue
WESLAKE ENGINEERING ENGLAND						
Britarms 2000 Mk3 Target pistol	·22 Short, ·22 LR	Blowback	Five	6″	Adjustable	Blue, Hard Chrome, Blue/hard chrome
WILDEY US						
	9mm Win Mag, ·45 Win Mag	Gas operated	Fourteen (9mm), Eight (·45)	6″, 7″, 8″, 10″	Adjustable	Stainless
WILKINSON US						
Sherry	·22 LR	Blowback	Eight	2⅛″	Fixed	Blue, Blue & gold
ZASTAVA YUGOSLAVIA						
Model 70	·32 Auto/7·65mm, ·380 Auto/9mmK	Blowback	Eight	3·7″	Fixed	Blue

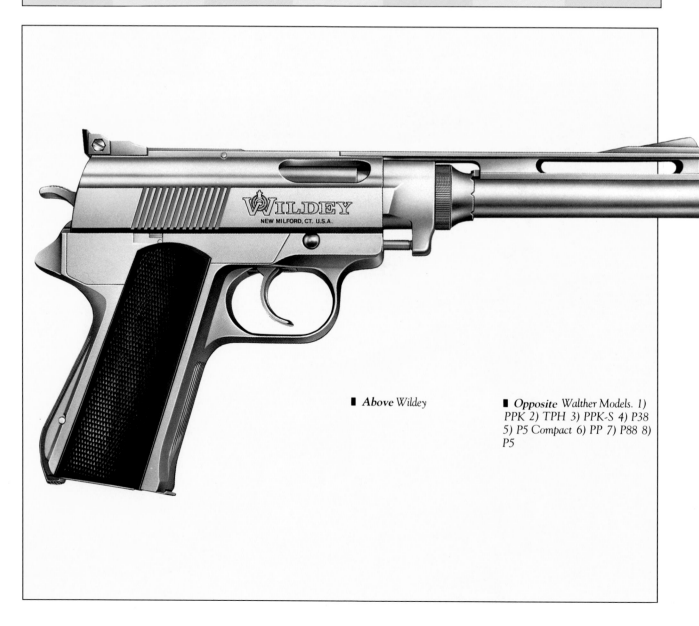

■ *Above* Wildey

■ *Opposite* Walther Models. 1) PPK 2) TPH 3) PPK-S 4) P38 5) P5 Compact 6) PP 7) P88 8) P5

ASSAULT PISTOLS

Assault pistols have been a curious development in exotic handguns during the 20th century. They fall midway between the compact pistols and revolvers used as sidearms, and full-blooded automatic machine pistols designed for offensive and defensive military use. Early attempts to produce fully automatic handguns by Browning and Mauser were not successful. The wheel has now turned full circle with modern assault pistols resembling military sub-machine guns (SMGs) – high capacity "stick" magazines which do not usually attach through the grip, straight blowback action, external cocking handles, sheet metal construction and utilitarian finish. Their inclusion in the market of domestic handguns derives from their ability to only work in the semi-automatic mode, usually firing from a closed bolt.

One of the world's most famous SMGs, the Israeli Uzi, has a smaller, closed-bolt brother, the UZI pistol, which retains the UZI line and character. Another famous SMG, the cheap and cheerful American MAC10 also has closed-bolt derivatives available for sale to civilians.

"Open bolt" service automatic weapons have a raised, solid striker set into the bolt face which ignites the cartridge as the breech closes, the weapon cycling continuously as long as the trigger is pressed. When released, the trigger acts by stopping the bolt flying forwards. Many fully automatic weapons have been converted to semi-automatic operation by fitting disconnectors and interrupters to the trigger mechanism. However, political fears of their reconversion to fully automatic fire make it far more acceptable to use a more complex "closed bolt" action, with a separate hammer/striker, floating firing pin and bolt disconnector. Closed bolt weapons can be manufactured to

fire selectively in fully automatic or burst fire modes, but it is extremely difficult to convert "semi-auto only" closed bolt firearms to selective fire.

Closed bolt weapons are inherently more accurate than similar open bolt versions since cartridge ignition is more consistent, and aim is not disturbed by the change in balance as the heavy bolt runs forwards on release of the trigger – as happens with open bolt guns.

Modern semi-automatic assault pistols are bulky when compared with more traditional handguns because their action usually works by straight blowback firing, high pressure cartridges like 9mm Luger and ·45 ACP. To cope with the pressures, a heavy bolt is used since its inertia prevents the breech opening too soon, and powerful springs are needed to control the travel of the bolt and return it to battery as it picks up a fresh round from the magazine.

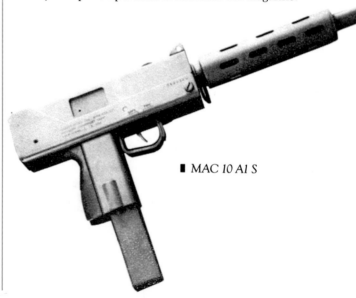

■ *MAC 10 A1 S*

■ *Bushmaster Auto Pistol*

■ *Calico P-900.*

■ **Top and above** Intratec TEC9

■ CALICO M-900

A radical innovation in design has come from the California Instrument Co. which produces the Calico carbine and assault pistol range. Originally made as the M-100P in ·22 LR, the Calico model M-900P pistol is available in 9mm Luger. What sets the Calico apart is the magazine design, which is helical and sits on top of the weapons receiver rather than below or to one side. The helical magazine, a cross between a drum and a tubular magazine, packs a vast amount of ammunition into a small space. Magazine options are for 50 or 100 rounds capacity of 9mm Luger cartridges. Space-age materials are used to keep weight down; the receiver is high tensile 356/T6 aircraft aluminium alloy. The action of the M-900P is roller-locked retarded blow-back, which means that a lightweight bolt can be used. The stock and grip is made from very strong, glass-filled polymer resin, as are the magazine housings, giving the pistol an unloaded weight of only 2¼lbs (just over 1kg). Loaded with 50 rounds, the 14 ins long, six ins-barrelled Calico M-900P pistol weighs just 2oz (60g) more than an **unloaded** ·357 Magnum Desert Eagle pistol, which has a magazine capacity of only (!) nine rounds. Loaded with 100 rounds, the weight of the M-900P increases to just under 6lbs (2.65kg) and the length becomes 19ins (483mm).

■ **Left and below** Derived from Israel Military Industries' legendary Uzi sub machine gun, the Uzi pistol is a compact semi-automatic assault pistol.

ASSAULT PISTOLS

All of the assault pistols listed are manufactured to fire only in the semi-automatic self-loading mode. All have fixed, drift adjustable or replaceable element sights.

Model	Calibre(s)	Type of action	Capacity	Barrel length(s)	Finish
BUSHMASTER US					
Auto Pistol	·223 Remington/ 5·56mm Nato	Gas operated	30	11½"	Blue, Electro Nickel
CALICO US					
M–100P & M-900P	·22 LR (M-100P), 9mm Luger (M-900P)	Roller locked retarded blowback	50, 100	6"	Black polymer resin
DEFENSE SYSTEMS INTERNATIONAL US					
M10A1S	9mm Luger, ·45 ACP	Closed bolt, blowback	32 (9mm), 30 (·45 ACP)	5·75"	Parkerized
ENCOM AMERICA US					
MP-9, MP-45, MkIV	9mm Luger (MP-9), ·45 ACP (MP-45 & MkIV)	Closed bolt	10, 30, 40, 50	4½", 6", 8", 10", 18", 18½" (interchangeable)	Black
FEDERAL ENGINEERING US					
XP-900 & XP-450	9mm Luger (XP-900), ·45 ACP (XP-450)	Closed bolt, blowback			Black steel
INTRATEC US					
Scorpion	·22 LR	Blowback	30	4"	Blue
Tec-9 & Tec-9S	9mm Luger	Closed bolt, blowback	36	5"	Matte blue (Tec-9), Stainless (Tec-9S)
ISRAEL MILITARY INDUSTRIES ISRAEL					
UZI Pistol	9mm Luger, ·45 ACP	Closed bolt, blowback	20, 25, 32	4½"	Black epoxy
WILKINSON ARMS US					
Linda	9mm Luger	Closed bolt, blowback	31	8·3"	Blue, black plastic grip, maple wood fore-end
ZASTAVA YUGOSLAVIA					
Spectre	9mm Luger	Closed bolt, blowback, trigger cocked	30	8"	

■ RIFLE AND CARBINE DERIVATIVES

Another way to produce an assault pistol is to cut down a rifle or carbine, and that is just what Bushmaster Firearms in the United States have done. By making extensive use of light aluminium alloys, Bushmaster has made a 5¼lb (2.3kg) 30 round magazine pistol based on the AK47-type gas-operated action which fires the ·223 Remington (5·56mm Nato) rifle cartridge through an 11½ ins barrel.

Before its financial collapse, Iver Johnson marketed the Enforcer Model 3000 pistol, which was little more than a cropped ·30 M1 carbine with a pistol grip. The American Military Arms Corporation, who has taken over Iver Johnson, do not currently list the Enforcer in its product range.

■ *Wilkinson Linda*

BLACK POWDER HANDGUNS

Black powder is a vintage propellant, an explosive mixture of charcoal, sulphur and potassium nitrate. It was used from the dawn of the firearms era to the end of the 19th century, when it was finally replaced by smokeless powders, mixtures of nitrocellulose and nitroglycerine. Black powder was not suited to automatic weapons because of its inefficient, low-pressure combustion and the thick acid residue it left behind on firing. The use of black powder in service revolvers also diminished for the same reasons, but the propellant was still used in muzzle-loading firearms as they could not cope with the pressures generated by smokeless powders.

Today, many firearms enthusiasts still enjoy shooting with percussion- and flint-ignited black powder handguns, and the lack of suitable genuine antique weapons has prompted Italian and American manufacturers to produce authentic replicas of early Colt, Remington, and Rodgers & Spencer revolvers. Some also produce kit form versions of early single barrelled flintlocks and percussion pistols, so that shooters can immerse themselves totally in their hobby.

International match target shooting takes place with muzzle-loaders, which are surprisingly accurate, and the search for greater accuracy has led to some very fine examples of pistolcraft: the West Germany 1858 Remington replica by Hege is better made and more expensive than many good quality centrefire pistols and revolvers.

The interest in muzzle-loading also prompted Ruger in the United States to make a "modern" black powder revolver based on its Blackhawk lockwork. The revolver also has adjustable sights and a cylinder spindle shroud to reduce fouling and jamming of the cylinder during extended shooting sessions.

The bulk of the replica revolvers are made in Italy by Uberti and Armi San Marco. Their sales are worldwide, and are very popular in France, who do not place the same restrictions on ownership of muzzle-loaders as they do on other handguns. Many replicas are made in stainless steel as well as in the traditional, blued carbon steel, as the effects of the acid corrosion on firing is not so marked on stainless steel.

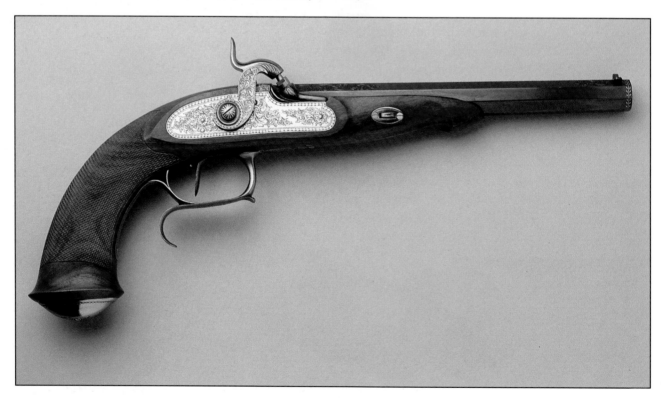

■ *Pedersoli Le Page replica*

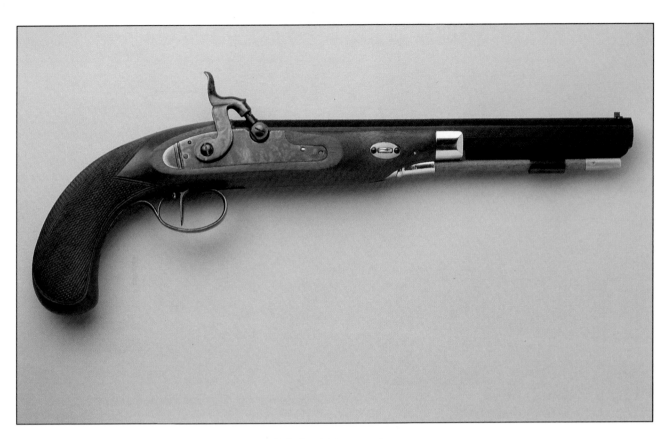

∎ *Pedersoli Manton replica*

∎ *Replica Le Mat percussion revolver*

PRINCIPAL MANUFACTURERS OF NEW BLACK POWDER HANDGUNS

Product range	Finishes available
ARMI SAN MARCO ITALY	
Replica percussion revolvers.	Blue, Stainless
FABBRICA ARMI FRATELLI PIETTA ITALY	
Replica Le Mat Revolver. This unique black powder revolver had formidable firepower in its day (1856), since it had nine ·44 chambers in the cylinder and an additional ·65″ barrel below the barrel.	Blue
HEGE WAFFENSCHMIEDE WEST GERMANY	
Replica Remington revolvers, Manton flintlock pistols	Corrosion inhibited carbon steel
HOPKINS & ALLEN US	
Replica underhammer boot pistols, calibres ·36 and ·45	Blue
DAVIDE PEDERSOLI ITALY	
Replica French, American & English single barrelled flintlock and percussion pistols & derringers. Texas Paterson revolvers	Blue
RUGER US	
"Old Army" revolvers, ·44 Cal, modern lockwork and target sights	Blue, Stainless
ALDO UBERTI ITALY	
Replica Colt percussion revolvers, Walker, Dragoons and 1851 Army in ·44 Cal, Navy Colts in ·36 Cal	Blue, Stainless in some models

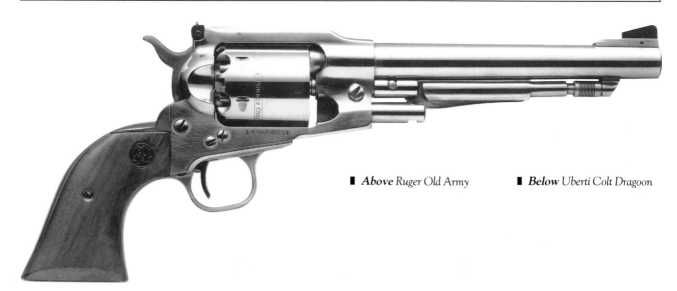

■ **Above** Ruger Old Army   ■ **Below** Uberti Colt Dragoon

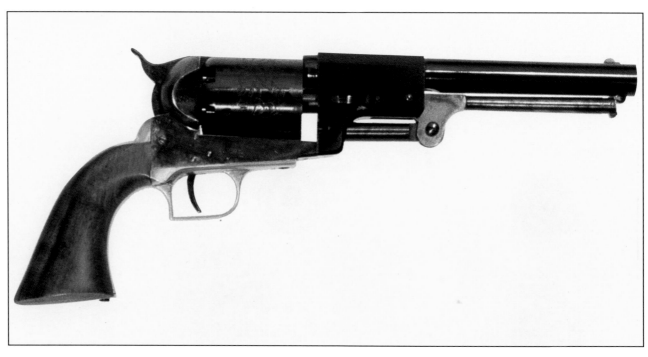

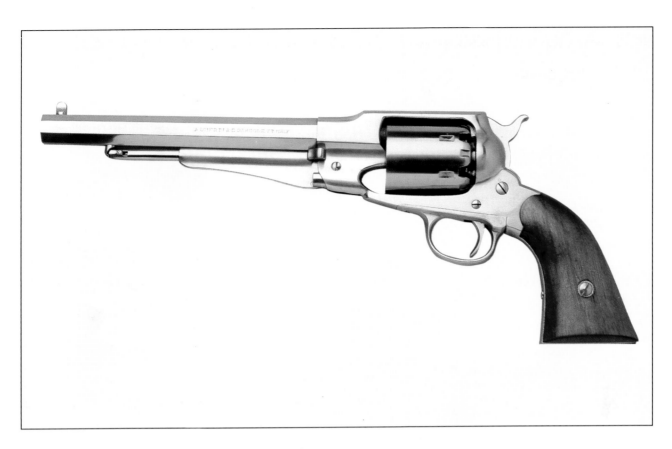

■ *Uberti Remington New Army*
replicas in stainless steel

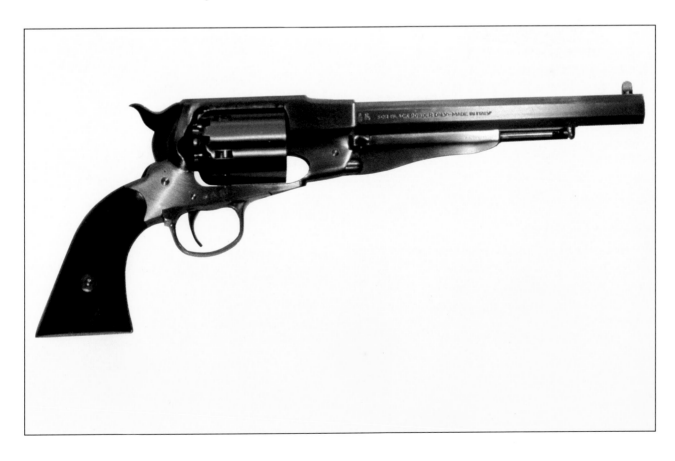

MANUFACTURERS FILE

■ **AMAC INC**
2202 Redmond Rd, Jacksonville, AR 72076, US

Pistols: 9mm Auto (9mmLu), TP22 (·22 LR), TP25 (·25 Auto/6.35 mm)

■ **AMERICAN ARMS NR**
Box 1055, Garden Grove, CA 92643, US

Eagle 380 (·380 Auto/9mmK)

■ **AMERICAN DERRINGER CORP**
127 N Lacey Dr., Waco, TX 76705, US

Derringer Model: 1 (·22 LR, ·22 WMR, ·22 Hornet, ·223/5·56mm, ·30 Lu, ·30–30 Win, ·32 AutoP/7·65mm, ·38 Sup, ·380 Auto/9mmK, ·38 Spl, 9mmU/9×18, 9mm Lu, 9mm Fed, ·357 Mag, ·357 Max, ·41 Mag, ·38–40, ·44–40 Win, ·44 Spl, ·44 Am, ·44 Mag, ·45 Colt, ·45 ACP, ·410 Gua-2½″), 3 (·38 Spl), 4 (·410 Gua-3″ &/or ·45 Colt, ·410 Gua-3″ plus ·45 Colt or ·45–70), 6 (·410 Gua-3″, ·45 Colt), 7 (·22 LR, ·32 S&W Lo, ·32 H&R Mag, ·380 Auto/9mmK, ·38 S&W, ·38 Spl, ·44 Spl), 10 (·38 Spl, ·45 ACP, ·45 Colt), 11 (·38 Spl), **Texas Commemorative** (·38 Spl, ·44–40, ·44 Am, ·45 Colt), **Semmerling LM-4** (9mmLu, ·45 ACP)

■ **AMT (ARCADIA MACHINE & TOOL)**
6226 Santon Diaz St, Irvindale, CA 91706, US

Government (·45 ACP), Hardballer (·45 ACP), Longslide (·45 ACP), Backup (·22 LR, ·380 Auto/9mmK), Automag II (·22 WMR)

■ **ANSCHUTZ**
Ulm/Donau, West Germany

Examplar Bolt Action Pistol (·22 LR, ·22 WMR)

■ **ARMI SAN MARCO**
Via Angelo Canossi 8, 25063 Gardone Val Trompia, Brescia, Italy

Replica percussion revolvers

■ **ARMINEX LTD**
10231 North Scottsdale Rd, B13, Scottsdale, AZ 85253, US

Pistols: Sleeping Beauty (·380 Auto/9mmK), new 9mm Pistol

■ **ARMINIUS – See WEIRAUCHT**

■ **ARMSCOR**
Philippines

38 Revolver (·38 Spl)

■ **ASTRA**
Unceta y Cia, Guernica, Spain

Pistols: A-90 (9mmLu, ·45 ACP), Constable (·22 LR, ·380 Auto/9mmK), A-60 (9mmLu, ·45 ACP)
Revolver Models: 44 (·44 Mag), 45 (·45 Colt), Terminator (·44 Mag), ·357 Magnum (·357 Mag)

■ **AUTO ORDNANCE CORP**
Williams Lane, West Hurley, NY 12491, US

ZG51 (·45 ACP), 1911A1 (·38 Sup, 9mmLu, ·41 AE, ·45 ACP)

■ **BENELLI ARMI SpA**
Via della Stazione 50, I 61029, Urbino, Italy

B76 Pistol (9mmLu)

■ **BERETTA**
Pietro Beretta SpA, 25063 Gardone Val Trompia, Brescia, Italy
Beretta USA, US

Pistols Models: 84 & 85 DA (·380 Auto/9mmK), 87BB (·22 LR), 950 BS (·22 Sh, ·25 Auto/6·35mm), 21 (·22 LR), 92F (9mmLu), 93R burst fire (9mmLu) (·22LR). Browning BDA (·380 Auto/9mmK)

■ **BERNADELLI**
Vincenzo Bernadelli SpA, Gardone Val Trompia, Brescia, Italy

Pistols: PO18 DA (9mmLu), PO18 Combat (9mmLu), Model 60 (·22 LR, ·32 Auto/7·65mm, ·380 Auto/9mmK), Model 69 (·22 LR), Model 68 (·22 Sh, ·22 L)

■ **BERSA**
Argentina

Pistols Models: 224 (·22 LR), Model 383 (·380 Auto/9mmK)

■ **BRNO**
Agrozet National Enterprise, Uhersky Brod, Czechoslovakia

Pistols: CZ 75 (9mmLu), CZ 85 (9mmLu), CZ 83 (·32 Auto/7·65mm, ·380 Auto/9mmK)
Drulov Target Pistols: Model 70, 75 (·22 LR)

■ **BROWNING US** Attn Paul Thompson
Rt 1, Morgan, UT 84050, US (part of International Browning organization distributing handguns made in Belgium, Italy and US)

Pistols: Buck Mark 22 Silhouette & Varmint (·22 LR)

■ **BUMBLE BEE WHOLESALE INC**
12521 Oxnard St, N Hollywood, CA 91606, US

Pocket Partner Pistol (·22 LR)

■ **BUSHMASTER FIREARMS CO**
999 Roosevelt Trail, Wyndham, ME 04062, US

Bushmaster Auto Pistol (·223/5·56mm)

■ **CALICO (CALIFORNIA INSTRUMENT CO)**
American Industries, 405 E 19th St, Bakersfield, CA
93305, US

Model 100-P Auto Pistol (·22 LR), M900 Pistol (9mmLu)

■ **CASPIAN ARMS LTD**
14 N Main St, Hardwick, VT 05843, US

Combat Competition Pistol (·45 ACP)

■ **CENTURY GUN DIST. INC**
1467 Jason Rd, Greenfield, IN 46140, US

Model 100 SA Revolver (·375 Win, ·444 Marlin, ·45–70)

■ **CHARTER ARMS CORP**
430 Sniffens Ln, Stratford, CT 06497, US

Revolvers: Bulldog (·44 Spl), Bulldog Pug (·44 Spl),
Bulldog Tracker (·357 Mag), Pathfinder (·22 LR, ·22
Mag), Pitbull (9mm Federal) Police Bulldog (·32 H&R
Mag, ·38 Spl), Police Undercover (·32 H&R Mag, ·38
Spl), Off-Duty (·38 Spl), Target Bulldog (·44 Spl),
Undercover (·32 S&W Lo, ·38 Spl)

■ **CHIPMUNK MFG INC**
114 E Jackson, PO Box 1104, Medford, OR 97501, US

Silhouette Pistol (·22 LR)

■ **COLT FIREARMS**
PO Box 1868, Hartford, CT 06101, US

Pistols: Gov't Mk IV/Series 80 (·45 ACP, ·38 Sup,
9mmLu), Delta Elite (10mm Auto), Combat Elite Mk
IV/Series 80 (·45 ACP), 380 Government Model (·380
Auto/9mmK), 380 Mustang (·380 Auto/9mmK), Mustang
Pocket Lite (·380 Auto/9mmK), Mustang Pocket II (·380
Auto/9mmK), Combat Commander (·45 ACP, ·38 Sup,
9mmLu), Lightweight Commander Mk IV/Series 80 (·45
ACP, ·38 Sup, 9mmLu), Officers ACP (·45 ACP)

Revolvers: DA – King Cobra (·357 Mag), Python (·357
Mag)
SA – Single Action Army (·44–40, 45 Colt)

■ **COMPETITION ARMS INC**
1010 S Plumer, Tucson, AZ 85719, US

Competitor Single Shot Pistol (·22 LR, ·223/5·56mm 7mm
TCV, 7mm Int, ·357 Max, ·41 Mag, ·44 Mag, ·454 Casull,
·375 Super Mag + Special Orders)

■ **COONAN ARMS INC**
830 Hampden Ave, St Paul, MN 55114, US

·357 Magnum Auto Pistol (·357 Mag)

■ **DAVIS INDUSTRIES**
13766 Arapahoe Pl, Chino, CA 91710, US

Derringer (·22 LR, ·22 WMR, ·25 Auto/6·35mm, ·32
Auto/7·65mm), P-32 Auto Pistol (·32 Auto/7·65mm)

■ **DEFENSE SYSTEMS INTERNATIONAL**
4321 Macland-Dallas Rd, Powder Springs, GA 30073, US

M10A1S Assault pistol (9mmLu, ·45 ACP)

■ **DETONICS**
New Detonics Mfg Corp, 13456 SE 27th Pl, Bellevue, WA
98005, US

Pistols: Combat Master MkVI/MkI (·45 ACP),
Servicemaster (·45 ACP), Scoremaster (·45 ACP, ·451
Detonics Mag)

■ **ENCOM AMERICA INC**
PO Box 5314, Atlanta, GA 30307, US

Assault Pistols: MP-9 (9mmLu), MP-45 (·45 ACP), Mk IV
(·45 ACP)

■ **ERMA**
West Germany

Pistols: KGP22 (Luger type) (·22 LR), KPG38 (·380
Auto/9mmK)

■ **FABBRICA ARMI FRATELLI PIETTA SNC**
Via Briggia 51, 25064 Gussago, BS Italy

Replica Le Mat black powder percussion revolver

■ **FABRIQUE NATIONAL D'ARMES DE GUERRE (FN)**
Herstale, Liege, Belgium (comm. dist. by Browning,
Belgium)

Pistols: High Power derivatives – Vigilante (9mmLu), MkII
(9mmLu), Sport (9mmLu), Competition (9mmLu)
Others – International (·22 LR), Practice 150 (·22 LR)

■ **FALCON FIREARMS MFG CORP**
PO Box 3748, Granada Hills, CA 91344, US

Portsider LH 1911 type ·45s

■ **FAS**
Via E. Fermi 8, 20019 Settimo, MI, Italy

601 (·22 Sh), 602 (·22 LR), 32 (·32, S&W Lo-WC)
Match Pistols

■ **FEDERAL ENG. CORP**
3161 N Elston Ave, Chicago, IL 60618, US

Assault Pistols: XP-900 (9mmLu), XP-450 (·45 ACP)

■ FEDERAL ORDNANCE
1443 Potrero Ave, El Monte, CA 91733, US

Ranger Pistol (·45 ACP)

■ FIREARMS IMPORT & EXPORT CORP
PO Box 4866, Hialeah Lakes, Hialeah, FL 33014, US

Texas Ranger Revolver – single action (·22 LR)

■ FREEDOM ARMS CO
PO Box 1776, Freedom, WY 83120, US

Casull five shot revolver (·454 Casull, ·45 Colt, ·44 Mag), Mini revolver (·22), Percussion Mini revolver (·22), Boot Gun

■ GAMBA SpA
Italy

Trident Match 900 revolver (·32 S&W Lo-WC, ·38 Spl), Mauser HSc 80G, 15 pistol (·32 Auto/7·65mm, 9mmU/9×18mm), SAB G 90 pistol (·30 Lu/7·65mm Lu, 9mmU/9×18mm)

■ GLOCK GmbH
Deutsch-Wagram, Vienna, Austria

Pistols: Glock 17 (9mmLu), 19 Compact (9mmLu), 17 L Competition (9mmLu)

■ GÖNCZ CO
11526 Burbank Blvd, #18 N. Hollywood, CA 91601, US

High-Tech Long Pistol Models GA, GS, GAT (9mmLu, ·30 Mau, ·38 Sup, ·45 ACP)

■ GRENDEL INC
PO Box 908, Rockledge, FL 32955, US

P-10 Pistol (·380 Auto/9mmK)

■ HÄMMERLI SPORTWAFFENFABRIK also see SIG/HÄMMERLI
CH-5600, Lensburg, Switzerland

Target pistols: Model 150 Free Pistol – single shot (·22 LR), Standard Models 208 & 211 (·22 LR), Model 232 Rapid Fire (·22 Sh), Model 280 (·22 LR, ·32 S&W Lo-WC) – carbon fibre construction

■ HECKLER AND KOCH GmbH
2738 Oberndorf am Neckar, West Germany

Pistols: P7K3 (·22LR, ·32 Auto/7·65mm, ·380 Auto/9mmK) P7-M8 (9mmLu), P7-M13 (9mmLu), P9S Target (9mmLu), P9S Combat (9mmLu), VP 70 – burst fire – (9mmLu)

■ HOLMES FIREARMS CORP
Rte 6, Box 242, Fayetteville, AR 72703, US

Assault Pistols: MP-83 (9mm Lu, ·45 ACP), MP-22 (·22 LR)

■ HOPKINS & ALLEN
3 Ethel Ave, PO Box 217, Hawthorne, NJ 07507, US

Underhammer Boot pistol (replica, black power calibres ·36 & ·45)

■ INTERARMS
10, Prince Street, Alexandria, VT 22313, US

Pistols: (under licence) Walther TPH (·22 LR), PPK (·380 Auto/9mmK)

■ INTRATEC INC
12405 SW 130th St, Miami, FL 33186, US

Assault Pistols: Tec-9 (9mmLu), Tec 9S (9mmLu) Assault Pistols
Derringer: Companion (·32 H&R Mag, ·38 Spl, ·357 Mag)
Pistol: Scorpion (·22 LR)

■ ISRAEL MILITARY INDUSTRIES
PO Box 1044, Ramat Hasharaon 47100, Israel

Pistols: Desert Eagle Gas Operated Self Loading Pistol (·357 Mag, ·44 Mag), UZI pistol (9mm)

■ ITHACA ACQUISITION CORPORATION
123 Lake Street, Ithaca, NY 14850, US

Single Shot Pistols: 20 X-Caliber (·22 LR, ·223/5·56mm, ·35 Rem, ·357 Mag, ·357 Max, ·44 Mag), 30 X-Caliber (·22 LR, ·223/5·56mm, ·35 Rem, ·357 Mag, ·357 Max, ·44 Mag)

■ ITM
Allmendstrasse 31, 4503 Solothurn, Switzerland

AT 84 Pistol (9mmLu, ·41 AE)

■ JENNINGS FIREARMS INC
PO Box 5416, Stateline, NV 89449, US

J-22 pistol (·22 LR)

■ KORRIPHILA GHBH
Postfach 103447, D6900 Heidelberg, West Germany

HSP 701 DA Auto pistol (9mmLu, ·38 Spl-Wc, ·38 Sup, ·45 ACP) Delayed roller lock action – limited production

■ KORTH
Willi Korth Sportwaffen-Herst, D-2418 Ratzeberg, West Germany

Semi-Automatic (9mmLu) Pistol. Revolver (·22 LR, ·22 Mag, ·32 S&W Lo, ·38 Spl, ·357 Mag, 9mmLu, 9×21 IMI)

■ LAR MNFG CO
4133 West Farm Rd, West Jordan, UT 84084, US

Grizzly pistols (·357 Mag, ·357/45 Grizzly win Mag, 10mm Auto, ·45 ACP, ·45 Win Mag)

■ LJUTIC IND. INC
PO Box 2117, 732 N 16th Ave, Yakima, WA 98907, US

LJ II Pistol, DA side by side barrels (·22 WMR)

■ LLAMA
Gabliono y Cia, Vitoria, Spain

Pistols: IX-A (·45 ACP), XI-B (9mmLu), Omni (9mmLu, ·45 ACP) Small Frame (·22 LR, ·32 Auto/7·65mm, ·380/9mmK)
Revolvers: Comanche III (·357 Mag), Comanche V (·357 Mag, ·44 Mag)

■ MANUFACTURE D'ARMES AUTOMATIQUE DE SAINT-ETIENNE
Saint-Etienne, France

French service pistol G1 (Beretta 92F) (9mmLu)

■ MANURHIN
Manufacture de Machines du Haut-Rhin (Manurhin), F-68060, Mulhouse-Bourtzwiller, France

Revolver MR 32 (·32 S&W Lo), MR 73 (·357 Mag & 9mmLu)

■ MAUSER-WERKE OBERNDORF
PO Box 1349, 7238 Oberndorf/Neckar, West Germany

Parabellum 08 Pistol (9mmLu) – Luger replica, MsC (9mmLu)

■ MAY OF LONDON
35 Cherry Tree Rise, Buckhurst Hill, Essex, England

Jurek ·22 Single Shot Target Pistol

■ MDA CORP
PO Box 185, Dayton, OH 45404, US

Maximum single shot falling block pistol (·22 Hornet – ·44 mag)

■ MKE
Makina ve Kimya Endustrisi Kurumu, Kirrikale, Ankara; Kirrikale Tûfek Fb, Istanbul, Turkey

Walther PP type Auto Pistol (·32 Auto/7·65mm & ·380 Auto/9mmK)

■ MORINI COMPETITION ARM SA
6814 Lamone, Switzerland

Model CM-80 Super Competition Pistol, single shot (·22 LR) CM100 Series

■ NAVY ARMS CO
689 Bergen Blvd, Ridgefield, NJ 07657, US

Luger Auto Pistol (·22 LR) Importers/manufacturers of replica flintlock and percussion pistols and revolvers

■ NEW ENGLAND FIREARMS INC
Industrial Row, Gardner, MA 01440, US

Harrington and Richardson Swing Out ·22 Revolvers

■ NORINCO
A7 Yuetan Nan Jie, Beijing, China

Pistols: Type 54 (7·62mm Tokarev) 64, 77 (7·62mm) 59 (9mmM) BS-01, SS-01, MS-01, PS-01 (·22 LR) Revolvers: ZS-01 (7·62mm Nagent)

■ NORTH AMERICAN ARMS
1800 North 300 West, Spanish Fork, UT 84660, US

450 Magnum Express Revolver (·450 Mag Exp, ·45 Win Mag), Mini-Revolvers (·22 Sh, ·22 LR, ·22 WMR)

■ PARDINI-FIOCCHI
Italy (imported to UK by Hull Cartridge Co)

Target Pistol (·22 LR)

■ DAVIDE PEDERSOLI
Via Artigiani 57, 25063 Gardone VT, Italy

Replica flintlock & percussion single barrelled pistols. Replica Texas Paterson revolver

■ RAVEN ARMS
1300 Bixby Dr, Industry, CA 91745, US

MP-25 Auto Pistol (·25/6·35mm)

■ REMINGTON ARMS CO
1007 Market Street, Wilmington, DE 19898, US

XP-100 Varmint Special (·223/5·56mm), XP-100 Custom Long Range Pistols (·223/5·56mm, 7mm-08, ·35 Rem)

■ ROCK PISTOL MFG (R&R SPORTING ARMS INC)
150 Viking Ave, Brea, CA 92621, US

XL Single Shot Pistol (formerly Merril) (·22 LR – ·45–70)

■ ROSSI
Amadeo Rossi, Metalurgica e Munições, Epifânio Fogaça, 143 PO Box 28, 93030 São Leopoldo RS Brazil

Revolvers: Models 42, 43, 483, 493, 511 (·22 LR), 20, 28, 89, 283, 293 (·32 S&W Lo), 27, 31, 33, 85, 851, 853, 854, 88, 881, 94, 941, 944, 95, 951, 953, 954 (·38 Spl) 97, 971, 974 (·357 Mag)

■ RUGER (STURM, RUGER & CO INC)
Lacey Place, Southport, CT 06490, US

Pistols: Mark II Standard (·22 LR), P-85 (9mmLu)

Revolvers: DA – GP100 (·357 Mag), Police Service-Six Models 108/708 (·38 Spl), Models 107/707 (·357 Mag), Speed-Six Models 208/738 (·38 Spl), Models 207/737 (·357 Mag), Redhawk (·41 Mag, ·44 Mag) Super Redhawk (·44 Mag)
SA – (NM = New Model) NM Blackhawk (·30 Car, ·38 Spl, ·357 Mag, ·41 Mag, ·44 Mag, ·45 Colt), NM Bisley (·357 Mag, ·41 Mag, ·44 Mag, ·45 Colt), NM Super Blackhawk (·44 Mag), Small Frame NM Bisley (·22 LR, ·32 H&R Mag), NM Super Single Six (·22 LR, ·22 WMR), NM Single Six (·32 H&R Mag)
BP – Old Army (·44 BP)

■ SAKO
Suojeluskuntain Asa-ja Konepajaoy, Finland

Triace Target Pistol (·22 Sh, ·22 LR, ·32 S&W Lo-WC)

■ SARDIUS INDUSTRIES LTD
12 Rokah Street, P.O. Box 644, Ramat-Gan, 52105 Israel

SD-9 Pistol (9mm Luger)

■ J P SAUER AND SOHN
Eckenforde, West Germany

SIG-Sauer Pistols: P-220 (9mmLu, ·38 Sup, ·45 ACP), P-225 (9mmLu), P-226 (9mmLu, ·38 Sup, ·45 ACP), P-230 (·32 Auto/7·65mm, ·380 Auto/9mmK)

■ SIG SWISS INDUSTRIAL COMPANY
Small Arms Division, CH-8212 Neuhausen Rhine Falls, Switzerland

SIG Pistols: P-210-2, P-210-6 (9mmLu)
SIG/Hämmerli Pistols: P-240 (·32 S&W Lo-WC) P-280 (·32 S&W Lo-WC)

■ SMITH & WESSON INC
2100 Roosevelt Ave, Springfield, MA 01101, US

Pistol Models: 41 (·22 LR), 52 (·38 Spl-WC), 422 (·22 LR), 439 (9mmLu), 459 (9mmLu), 469 (9mmLu), 639 (9mmLu), 645 (·45 ACP), 659 (9mmLu), 669 (9mmLu), 745 (·45 ACP)

Revolver Models: 10 Military and Police (·38 Spl), 13 Military and Police Heavy Barrel (·357 Mag), 15 Combat Masterpiece (·38 Spl), 17 K-22 Masterpiece (·22 LR), 19 Combat Magnum (·357 Mag), 25 (·45 Colt), 27 (·357 Mag), 29 (·44 Mag), 31 Regulation Police (·32 S&W Lo), 34 1953 ·22/32 Kit Gun (·22 LR), 36 Chiefs Specials (·38 Spl), 37 Chiefs Special Airweight (·38 Spl), 38 Bodyguard Airweight (·38 Spl), 49 Bodyguard (·38 Spl), 57 (·41 Mag), 60 Chiefs Special Stainless (·38 spl), 63 1977 ·22/32 Kit Gun Stainless (·22 LR), 64 Military and Police (·38 Spl), 65 Military and Police Heavy Barrel (·357 Mag), 66 Combat Magnum (·357 Mag), 67 Combat Masterpiece (·38 Spl), 581 Distinguished Service Magnum (·357 Mag), 586 Distinguished Combat Magnum (·357 Mag), 624 (·44 Spl), 629 (·44 Mag), 649 Bodyguard (·38 Spl), 657 (·41 Mag), 681 Distinguished Service Magnum (·357 Mag), 686 Distinguished Combat Magnum (·357 Mag)

■ SOKOLOVSKY CORP
PO Box 70113, Sunnyvale, CA 94086, US

45 Automaster Pistol (·45 ACP)

■ SPRINGFIELD ARMOURY INC
420 W Main St, Geneseo, IL 61254, US

1911-A1 pistol (·38 Sup, 9mmLu, ·45 ACP), Omega Pistol (1911 frame, Peters Stahl Omega slide, interchangeable barrels, ·38 Sup, 10mm Auto, ·45 ACP)

■ STAR
B Echeverria, Eibar, Spain

Pistols: 30M, 30PK, BM, BKM (all 9mmLu), PD (·45 ACP), 22FR (·22 LR)

■ STEEL CITY ARMS INC
PO Box 81926, Pittsburgh, PA 15217, US

Pistols: FR (·22 LR), Double Deuce (·22 LR, ·25 Auto/6·35mm), War Eagle (9mmLu)

■ STEYR
Steyr-Daimler-Puch AG, Postbox 1000, A-4400, Steyr, Austria

Steyr GB pistol (9mmLu)

■ SUPER SIX LTD
PO Box 266, Elkhorn, WI 53121, US

Golden Bison 45–70 Revolver (·45–70) (Manganese bronze frame)

■ GUISEPPE TANFOGLIO
Gardone Val Trompia, Italy

Tanarmi SA Revolver Model TA76 (·22 LR, ·22 WMR), O/U Derringer (·38 Spl).
Pistols: GT32 (·32 Auto/7·65mm), GT380 (·380 Auto/9mmK), GT380XE (·380 Auto/9mmK), GT27 (·32 Auto/7·65mm)

■ FRATELLI TANFOGLIO
Gardone Val Trompia, Brescia, Italy

TA 90 Pistol (9mmLu)

■ TAURUS
Forjas Taurus SA, Porto Alegre, Brazil

Pistols: PT-92AF (9mmLu), PT-99AF (9mmLu)
Revolvers: 66 (·357 Mag), 73 (·32 S&W Lo), 80 (·38 Spl), 82 (·38 Spl), 83 (·38 Spl), 85 (·38 Spl)

■ TEXAS LONGHORN ARMS INC
PO Box 703, Richmond, TX 77469, US

Texas Longhorn single action revolvers ("all centrefire calibres"), Jezebel single shot pistols (·22 Sh, ·22 L, ·22 LR)

■ THOMPSON-CENTER ARMS
PO Box 2426, Rochester, NH 03867, US

Contender single shot pistol (twenty-two calibres available)

■ ALDO UBERTI
Via G. Carducci 41, Ponte Zanano (Brescia), Italy

Pistols: Rolling Block single shot (·22 LR, ·22 WMR, ·357 Mag)
Revolvers: DA – Inspector (·32 S&W Lo. ·38 Spl),
SA – Phantom (·357 Mag, ·44 Mag), 1873 Cattleman (·22 LR, ·22 WMR, ·38 Spl ·357 Mag, ·44–40 Win, ·45 Colt) 1873 Buckhorn (·44 40, ·44 Mag), 1873 Buntline (·357 Mag, ·44–40 Win, ·44 Mag, ·45 Colt), 1873 Stallion (·22 LR/·22 WMR convertible 1875 Army (·357 Mag, ·44–40 Win, ·45 Colt), 1890 Army (·357 Mag, ·44–40 Win, ·45 Colt)
BP – Walker 1847 (·44 BP), 1st Model Dragoon (·44 BP), 2nd Model Dragoon (·44 BP), 3rd Model Dragoon (·44 BP), Army 1851 (·44 BP), 1861 Navy (cal? ·36?), 1862 Pocket Navy (·36 BP)

■ ULTRA LIGHT ARMS
PO Box 1270, Granville Way, WV 26534, US

Model 20 Reb Hunter's Pistol (·22–250 to ·308. Most calibres available on request)

■ UNIQUE
Manufacture d'Armes des Pyrenees, Côte Basque, France

DES 69 Target Pistol (·22 Sh, ·22 LR), DES 32 (·32 S&W Lo-WC), DES/823 U (·22 Sh) 1

■ USSR
9mm Makarov Pistol (PH)x (9mm Makarov), Pistolet Samozarjadni Malogbarythyj Pistol (5·45mm), Margolin MC (Vostock) Standard Pistol (·22 LR), Margolin MCU Rapid Fire (·22 Sh), TOZ-35 Free Pistol (·22 LR), TOZ-36 Revolver (7·62mm Nagant), TOZ-49 Revolver (7·62mm Sh)

■ VICTORY ARMS CO LTD
5 Owl Close, Moulton Park, Northampton, England

Victory Pistol (9mm, ·38 sup, ·41 AE, ·45 ACP)

■ CARL WALTHER GmbH
7900 Ulm, West Germany

Pistols: PP (·22 LR, ·32 Auto/7·65mm, ·380 Auto/9mmK), PPK (·380 Auto/9mmK), PPK/S (·380 Auto/9mmK), P-38 (·22 LR, 9mmLu, TPH (·22 LR), P-88 (9mmLu), Free Pistol single shot (·22 LR), GSP (·22 LR, ·32 S&W Lo-WC), OSP (·22 Sh)

■ HERMANN WEIRAUCH KG
Postfach 20, 8744 Mellrichstadt, West Germany

Arminius Revolvers – Double Action: HW3, 5, 5T, 7, 7T, 68 (·22 LR, ·22 WMR, ·32 S&W Lo), HW7 S, 9, 9ST (·22 LR), HW 38, 38 T (·38 Spl), HW 357, 357 T, 357 Match (·357 Mag).
Arminius Revolvers – Single Action: ARM 3575, 3576 T, 3577 (·357 Mag), ARM 445, 446 T, 447 (·44 Mag), ARM 455, 456 T, 457 (·45 Colt)

■ WESLAKE ENGINEERING
Sleaford Service Station, Nr Bordon, Hampshire, England

Britarms 2000 Mk 3 target pistol (·22 Sh, ·22 LR)

■ DAN WESSON ARMS
293 Main Street, Monson, MA 015057, US

Revolver Models: 40 Silhouette (·357 Mag), 41V (·41 Mag), 44V (·44 Mag), 22 (·22 LR), 8–2 (·38 Spl), 9–2 (·38 Spl), 14–2 (·357 Mag), 15–2 (·357 Mag), 32M (·32 H&R Mag)

■ WICHITA ARMS
444 Ellis, Wichita, KS 67211, US

Single Shot Pistols: MK-40 Silhouette (·22–250, 7mm IHMSA, ·308 WCF/7·62×51mm), Silhouette (·22–250, 7mm IHMSA, ·308 WCF/7·62×51mm), Hunter International (·22 LR, ·22 Mag, 7mm Int-R, ·30–30 Win, ·32 H&R Mag, ·357 Mag, ·357 Max), Classic (any calibre up to and including ·308 WCF7, 62×51mm)

■ WILDEY
28 Old Route 7, Brookfield, CT 06804, US

Wildey Pistol (9mm WinMag, ·45 WinMag)

■ WILKINSON ARMS
26884 Pearl Rd, Parma, ID 83660, US

Linda Assault Pistol (9mmLu), Sherry pistol (·22 LR)

■ ZAVODI CRVERNA ZASTAVA
Beograd, Yugoslavia

Closed bolt DA assault pistol – Spectre (9mmLu), Zastava Mod 70 pistol (·32 Auto/7·65mm, ·380/9mmK)

GLOSSARY

ACP
Abbreviation for cartridge designation "Automatic Colt Pistol".

ACTION
Generalized description of part or all of a firearm's mechanism concerned with loading and/or firing. e.g. "bolt action", "martini action".

AE
Abbreviation for cartridge designation "Action Express".

AUTO
1 Suffix to cartridge designation indicating that the round is designed for use in self-loading pistols.
2 Shortened form of "automatic" which is often applied to self-loading pistols. These are generally "semi-automatic" rather than "fully automatic".

AUTO MAG
Brand name for high powered self-loading pistols and ammunition originally made during the early 1970s. The name is perpetuated on a .22 gas assisted pistol produced by AMT in America.

AUTO-RIM
Cartridge designation for a thick rimmed ·45in revolver round designed to fit the chambers of a revolver which had originally been made to fire ·45 ACP pistol ammunition using securing clips.

BLACK POWDER
Also known as gunpowder. Black powder is a mixture of potassium nitrate, charcoal and sulphur in the approximate proportions of 75:15:10. The earliest form of reliable propellant known, it was in common use from the dawn of firearms until the end of the 19th century. Still used in antique and replica "muzzle loading" weapons, but has been superseded by nitrocellulose based propellants for modern handguns.

BLOWBACK
Operating method of small calibre self-loading pistols. The breech block is held closed by spring pressure which with the inertia of the breech block holds the cartridge in the chamber of the barrel on firing. Once inertia is overcome by recoil, the breech moves back freely controlled by the recoil spring, ejecting the fired case and loading a fresh cartridge into the chamber.

BLUEING
Also known as 'blacking'. Controlled corrosion of the surface of ferrous steel which results in a thin inert blue/black surface layer offering some protection against further corrosion.

BOLT ACTION
Description of a firearm loading mechanism which uses a manually operated bolt to lock the cartridge in the chamber.

BOTTLENECKED
Description of a cartridge which steps down to a smaller diameter from the base of the case to the neck. Usually seen in rifle ammunition, but also used in a few self-loading pistol calibres.

BREAKTOP
Revolver or pistol which is loaded or unloaded by unlatching the barrel and chamber/cylinder and swinging it down to open the breech. Typical examples are the Webley revolvers and Thompson/Center Contender pistols.

BROOMHANDLE
Nickname given to the Mauser Model C1896 pistol which had a distinctive wooden butt.

BULLETT
Shaped projectile fired from a firearm. Generally made from a lead alloy and often covered with a copper or steel coating for use in high velocity ammunition. "Bullet" does not refer to a complete round of ammunition.

BURST FIRE
Trigger mechanism which permits firing of more than one round of ammunition with each pull of the trigger. Interrupters stop each burst after a preset number of rounds such as two or three. Burst fire must not be confused with fully automatic fire which will only stop when the trigger is released or the magazine emptied.

CALIBRE
1 Measurement of the bore of a firearm made across the lands of the rifling. It is the bore of the barrel minus the depth of the rifling grooves.
2 Name given to cartridge designation of a weapon and ammunition which may or may not be the same as the exact bore of the firearm (see nomenclature in Chapter 3).

CARTRIDGE
Complete round of ammunition comprising case, primer, propellant and bullet.

CENTREFIRE (CENTERFIRE)
Cartridges which have a central primer or percussion cap in the end of the cartridge case.

CHAMBER
Part of the barrel or cylinder which contains the cartridge on firing.

CYLINDER
Major component of a revolver which hold the cartridges and brings them in line with the barrel as the hammer/trigger is cocked.

DAGG
Name given to early wheel lock pistols.

DELAYED BLOWBACK
Mechanism for preventing the breech block opening in a self-loading weapon until the bullet has left the barrel and the breech pressure has dropped. Most common is the Browning delayed blowback system which keeps the barrel locked into the slide with lugs until the pressure drops whereupon the barrel cams down and permits the slide to cycle by blowback (*qv*).

DERRINGER
Originally a large bore single shot pistol sold by Philadelphia gunsmith Henry Deringer. The name has been corrupted to derringer and is most commonly used to describe small two shot handguns (see Chapter 6).

DISCONNECTOR
Internal device in a self loading weapon which prevents fully automatic fire and necessitates the release of the trigger before firing subsequent shots.

DOUBLE ACTION (DA)
Description of trigger mechanism which can be cocked and fired by pulling the trigger or can be manually cocked by pulling back the hammer which results in a lighter trigger pull. Also applied to the trigger cocking shooting method.

FLINTLOCK
17th Century firearm ignition system in which a flint clamped in a swinging arm was propelled by spring pressure against a steel. This resulted in a shower of sparks which ignited fine black powder placed in a "pan" which in turn ignited the main propellant charge.

FLOBERT
Early rimfire type cartridge design where priming compound covered all of the inside of the cartridge case base.

GALLING
Effect of two similar metals rubbing against each other

resulting in surface damage and mechanical fusion.

GAS OPERATION
Method of cycling a self loading firearm using the propellant gases to push back the breech.

GLASER
Brand name for special "Safety Slug" ammunition designed for personal defence.

HANDCANNON
Brand name for Thompson/Center Contender pistols which have been converted by SSK Industries to fire very high powered ammunition for hunting or silhouette shooting.

HANDLOAD
Home manufacture of ammunition by a shooter. Handloading is used to tailor the ammunition to the characteristics of the firearm and the use to which it is put. Handloading can increase accuracy and alter the power of a weapon.

HEADSPACE
Distance between the base of the cartridge and the face of the breech. Also used to refer to the reference point at which the cartridge is located in the chamber. For revolvers this is usually the rim at the base of the cartridge, for self loading pistols this is often the mouth of the case at the front of the chamber.

HOLLOWPOINT
Bullet design with a hollow nose which is designed to expand and mushroom on impact giving greater shock effect. Sometimes erroneously referred to as "Dum Dums".

INVESTMENT CASTING
Fine tolerance method of casting metals using an injection moulded wax positive form of the final product to create a negative ceramic mould. Results in minimal machining and lower costs in high volume production.

IPSC
International Practical Shooting Confederation, international controlling body for one type of action or combat style target shooting.

KENGIL
Brand name for a British single shot pistol used for long range target shooting.

MAGNUM
Originally a cartridge suffix used to denote powerful high pressure ammunition. Now appears on some new low pressure calibres as a marketing ploy rather than an indication of terminal effectiveness. The original Magnums, ·357 and ·44 have been overtaken in the power league by the Maximums, Supermags and Casull calibres.

MAJOR CALIBRE
High scoring band designated by the IPSC for shooters using ammunition where the product of the bullet weight in grains and velocity in feet per second, divided by 1000 is equal to or greater than 175. Based on the momentum of a 230 grain ·45 ACP bullet when fired from a 4″ barrelled pistol.

MINOR CALIBRE
Low scoring band designated by the IPSC for shooters using ammunition where the product of the bullet weight in grains and velocity in feet per second, divided by 1000 is equal to or greater than 125. Originally derived from the momentum of ·38 Special revolver ammunition, it is now based on the momentum of a 115 grain 9mm Luger bullet when fired from a 4″ barrelled pistol.

MULTI CALIBRE
Brand name for a conversion to the Colt 1911 pistol by Peters-Stahl in West Germany which permits different calibre barrels and ammunition to be used with the same frame and slide.

MUZZLE ENERGY
Energy of a bullet when it leaves a firearm barrel. Calculated in foot-pounds from the square of the velocity multiplied by the bullet weight in pounds divided by twice the acceleration due to gravity. Since the acceleration due to gravity is a constant, the equation can be reduced to $ME = (V^2 \times BW)/450240$.

MUZZLE LOADING
Method of loading weapons with chambers or barrels closed at one end. Propellant is poured down into the chamber and the bullet or ball projectile rammed down on top. Ignition can be by flint, match, wheel, or percussion cap. Muzzle loaders use low pressure black powder or its substitutes rather than modern high pressure products as propellants.

MUZZLE VELOCITY
Speed of bullet when it leaves a firearm's barrel. Measured in feet per second (fps) or metre per second (mps).

NITROCELLULOSE
Base material for modern high pressure non corrosive propellant. Nitrocellulose is mixed with retardants and sometimes nitroglycerine to modify its burning rate and give greater versatility in different weapons.

PEACEMAKER
Alternative name for Colt's Single Action Army model revolver first made in 1872.

PEPPERBOX
Repeating handguns from early in the 19th Century. In effect they were revolvers without a barrel, each chamber being elongated to form a short integral barrel without rifling. Rendered obsolete by the introduction of Colt's revolver, they were still popular until the American Civil War when their production finally ceased.

PERCUSSION
Name given to the explosive effect of certain salts when struck. When the salts are contained in thin copper cup the result is a percussion cap which is placed on a nipple of a black powder firearm. Modern primers are also a type of percussion cap which form an integral part of a cartridge.

PINFIRE
Early metallic cartridge type which had a percussion cap contained inside the cartridge which was detonated by a pin which extended out of the case.

POWER FACTOR
Name given to the result of the IPSC major and minor calibre calculation.

POWER FLOOR
Minimum power level for IPSC major and minor power ratings.

PRIMER
Impact sensitive percussion cap used in centrefire ammunition which is inserted into the centre of the cartridge base. Ignites the main propellant charge when struck.

PROPELLANT
Principal consumable component of ammunition. When ignited, propellants burn at a very high rate generating high pressure gas. The gas propels the bullet out of the cartridge case and up the barrel of the firearm.

PYRITE
Yellow mineral formed from sulphur and iron which was used to create sparks in wheel lock ignition.

REVOLVER
Handgun type which has a fixed barrel and a revolving cylinder. The cylinder brings the ammunition in line with barrel as the hammer is cocked.

RIFLING
Helical grooves inside a firearm barrel which impart stabilising spin to a bullet as it travels down the bore.

RIMFIRE
Cartridge type in which the priming compound is located in the thin rim of the cartridge case base. One of the first metallic cartridge types, still popular today for target shooting and pest control.

ROLLER LOCKED
Method of creating delayed blowback in self loading weapons by locking the breech with rollers until chamber pressure drops.

ROUND
Single unit of ammunition also called a cartridge.

SELFLOADING
Description of an action type which when fired, automatically ejects the spent case, recocks the hammer and chambers a fresh cartridge.

SINGLE ACTION
Also known as hammer cocking in revolvers where it is necessary to thumb back the hammer in order to index the cylinder and prepare the revolver for firing. Applied to self loading pistols which cannot be fired by trigger cocking.

SMALLBORE
General description of firearms which chamber ·22″ rimfire ammunition.

SMOKELESS POWDER
Propellant type based on nitro cellulose which was introduced at the turn of the 20th Century. Produces considerably less smoke and residue than black powder.

SNAPHAUNCE
Early type of flint lock.

TOGGLE LOCK
Barrel locking system used in Maxim machine guns which was adapted by Borchardt and Luger for their self loading pistols.

TRIGGER COCKING
Method of firing a handgun where pulling the trigger cocks then fires the piece. Incorrectly known as "double action", since many handguns have been made which can only fire when trigger cocked and hence are a form of single action.

UZI
Brand name for Israel Military Industries self loading pistols and machine guns, from the original designer's name.

WADCUTTER
Bullet design used for target shooting which has a flat front and a long bearing surface for stability at low velocities.

WHEEL LOCK
First reliable firearm ignition system dating from the 16th Century in which a steel wheel is spun against iron pyrites to create sparks for propellant ignition.

WMR
Abbreviation for Winchester Magnum Rimfire, a ·22″ cartridge designation.

INDEX

ACKNOWLEDGEMENTS

The author and publishers would like to thank the following for providing information, photographs and data: Frank C Barnes, Birmingham Proof House, Browning Sports Ltd, Coach Harness (UK Uberti and Pedersoli agents), Conjay (UK IMI agents), Edgar Brothers (UK BRNO and Star agents), Framar Shooting World (UK Hämmerli agents), Oliver Gower (UK FAS agent), *Gun Digest* (USA), *Guns Review* (UK). *Guns and Weapons Magazine,* John Harness (Hilton Gun Co), Ian V Hogg, Walter J Howe (Shooting Industry Reports), Modern and Antique Firearms (Kengil), Mountain and Sowden, Pro Gun Services, Shooting Developments (Morini agents), John Smart, Jan Stevenson *(Handgunner), Target Gun,* Victory Arms.

A host of individuals kindly loaned their own handguns for photography, including: Alan Arnsby; Linda, Andrew and Tony Baldwin; Bob and Barbara Barber; Martin Barber; Tony and Yve Cattermole; Gary Clark; Peter Foulkes; Malcolm Hinds; Arthur Hull; Leyton James; Phil James; Nigel Jennings; John Keener; Sandy McNab; Bill Martin; John Parry; Steve Parsons; Rodger Saunders; Frank Sitton; John Smart.

In addition, thanks are due to the many manufacturers worldwide (listed in the Manufacturers File) who supplied invaluable information and pictures.